Right Place, Right Time

The "TRUE" story of my life (at least in my own mind) from October 28, 1955 through the present time!

Part 2

KEVIN DWARES

Right Place, Right Time, Part 2
Copyright © 2025 Kevin Dwares

Produced and printed by Stillwater River Publications.
All rights reserved. Written and produced in the
United States of America. This book may not be reproduced
or sold in any form without the expressed, written
permission of the author(s) and publisher.

Visit our website at
www.StillwaterPress.com
for more information.

First Stillwater River Publications Edition.

ISBN: 978-1-965733-14-1

1 2 3 4 5 6 7 8 9 10
Written by Kevin Dwares.
Cover & interior book design by Matthew St. Jean.
Published by Stillwater River Publications,
West Warwick, RI, USA.

Names: Dwares, Kevin, author.
Title: Right place, right time : the "true" story of my life
(at least in my own mind) from October 28, 1955 through the
present time! Part 2 / Kevin Dwares.
Other titles: Right place, right time. Part 2
Description: First Stillwater River Publications edition. |
West Warwick, RI, USA : Stillwater River Publications, [2025]
Identifiers: ISBN: 978-1-965733-14-1
Subjects: LCSH: Dwares, Kevin. | Near-death experiences. |
Loss (Psychology) | Grief. | Judaism. | Introspection. |
Conduct of life. | God--Will. | Rhode Island--Biography. |
LCGFT: Autobiographies. | Humor. | BISAC: BIOGRAPHY &
AUTOBIOGRAPHY / Memoirs. | HUMOR / Form / Essays.
Classification: LCC: F85 .D93 2025 |
DDC: 974.5044092--dc23

*The views and opinions expressed in this book are solely
those of the author(s) and do not necessarily reflect the
views and opinions of the publisher.*

*Dedicated to Barbara Gold Dwares, the love of my life.
I Love You Barbara (Baba) and I always will.*

CONTENTS

Preface ix

Origin of *Right Place, Right Time Part 2*
Sixty-Eight Years in the Making xi

Anti-Semitism: It's All Around Us
Don't Call Me Doc Again—Bridge (1972) 1
Sean O'Brien and Hitler Comments (1985 – 1987) 5
Pool in Florida - I Jew'd Him Down (2001) 8

Automobile Incidents
Handkerchief Story (1966) 10
Locking Keys in Station Wagon and Dad Was Mad (1966) 12
Station Wagon Hit Broadside in Downtown
Providence (1967) 14

Death and Other Health Issues
Dad Arrested After Finding Body at Narragansett Town
Beach (1967) 16
Family (Deaths, Births, and Anniversaries as of 2024) 18

Hospital
The Nurse and Gun in Mouth (1980) 21
Kevin Having Thyroid Surgery. Barbara Looking for
Dog (2005) 24
Telephone in Pre-Operating Room During (2007)
Disk Surgery 25

Lessons in Life
　Bomb Under the Car (1976) — 28
　Know the correct street in Brooklyn, New York (1979) — 29
　Woman on Train (1990) — 32
　What Max Gold Dwares Wrote About His Jewish Faith
　　While Battling Cancer (2001) — 34
　French Drains (2024) — 37
　Lost and Found (Saint Anthony's Prayer) — 42
　Lost Earring—Sedona. (1995) — 44
　Max Bracelet (2006) — 44
　Lost Wallets—Price Rite (2020) / Walgreens (2022) — 46
　Lost Wallet—Price Rite (2020) — 46
　Lost Wallet—Walgreens (2022) — 47

Medical and Health Issues
　Seven New Teeth (2023) — 49
　More Gum Issues—Take a Bite out of That (2024) — 50

Meeting Famous People
　Richard Nixon (1960) — 52
　Meeting Lorne Greene (1965) — 53
　Muhammad Ali, (1978) — 53
　President Jimmy Carter and Dinner at Mainelli's (1985) — 55
　Meeting President George H.W. Bush 41st U.S.
　　President (1989) — 58
　Jack Klugman (Washington D.C.) (1999) — 60
　Meeting President George W. Bush 43rd U.S. President (2007) — 60
　Meeting Jay Leno (2018) — 61
　Meeting Jesus or a Lookalike (2019) — 63

Meeting the Woman Who Would Change My World
　Meeting Barbara Due to the Connections with Sheryl
　　(Marks) Ishai — 65

First Date at Bowling Alley Breakfast (March 11, 1979)   66
Second Date at Bowling Alley Breakfast (June 30, 2024)   68

Money, Money, Money
Insurance Scam $10,000 Engagement Ring at Golf Driving Range (1975)   70
Boat Insurance Fraud (1976)   71
Paying Off Mortgage (1990)   73
Attempted Boat Sinking—Wealthy Doctor (2000)   75
Gambling $1,800 Twice and $700 with Max (2002)   77

Shekels—Monetary Unit of Israel/US Dollar
2001 Gansett Ave Cranston (Boston Sub)   81
2010 Gansett Ave Cranston (Disney Trip)   81
2013—Savers ($85 Find)   82
Splitting the Bill (2018)   84
Statue of Liberty (Follow-Up 2023)   85
Noises We All Hear and Ignore: From Birth to Death and Beyond   86

Stolen Items
Delivering Bags of Furs (1975)   88
Missing Fishing Rod (1975)   89
The Stolen Glove (From a Young Boy Until the Present Time)   92

Stupid and Dumb Incidents
Handbag Robbery Thayer Street (1970)   94
Shooting at Building (1971)   95

Up, Up, and Away
Flying with J.B. (1993)   98
Test Flight on Apache Helicopter Vomiting (1999)   101
Parachute with Max (August 11, 2002)   103

World Problems or Just Everyday Issues
    Irving Avenue Stories (1980-1985)—Our First Apartment   108
    Packard Street Stories 1985-2017—Our First Home   111
    A Few More Packard Street Stories   112
    Balsam Court Stories (2017-Present) Our Second and Hopefully Final Home.   113
    June 2018   115
    March 2019   116
    May 2, 2023   117
    Hot Water Heater Replacement May 24, 2023   118

World Problems—At Least in My Own Mind
    Tomato "Capers" (Ongoing)   119

The Spelling of the Word G-D   124

My Final Thoughts   125

What The Truth Means When Telling Stories "Right Place, Right Time"   130

Acknowledgements   *134*
About the Author   *135*

PREFACE

I started this book on Sunday January 7, 2024 but have been going over my numerous notebooks for about two years. This book is actually a continuation of my prior book entitled *Right Place, Right Time*.

It's hard to believe myself, that in my life I have personally experienced many different types of incidents that ranged from anti-Semitism, automobile accidents, death, life lessons, finding lost items, medical and health issues, meeting the woman who would change my life, money issues, stupid and dumb things, flying high and many more.

As you read my book you will notice that I have been at the right place and the right time during my life. I also would like to say that writing this has also been very good for me personally as it has allowed me to get some things out that had been bottled up for many years. It has been therapeutic for me. The stories are all part of where I came from and have shaped me into the man I have become.

The reader may also enjoy a few additional stories about my life under the paragraphs entitled "World Problems." Everyone has numerous issues to deal with on a daily basis as I do, and I have included these as well.

So, sit back, relax, and buckle in as you begin to read a few additional (fifty-seven) short stories of my life and me being at the Right Place at the Right Time.

ORIGIN OF *RIGHT PLACE, RIGHT TIME PART 2*

Sixty-Eight Years in the Making

For many years I had dreams about my father passing away at the age of forty on February 19, 1968. As many of you know it may seem highly unlikely, but my late son Max Gold Dwares passed away at the young age of twenty after battling chronic myelogenous leukemia on February 18, 2004. Max's funeral was on the same day, February 19, that my dad died on thirty-six years earlier. Is it a coincidence or was it meant to be? We may never know unless G-d himself reveals secrets to us as we venture out of this earthly life into heaven or hell.

I had thought of numerous titles to my book such as "It Could Be Meant to Be," and "Right Place, Right Time, the Conclusion." I immediately eliminated that second one because one's life only truly concludes when they pass on. Since I am in no hurry to leave my wonderful family and life that G-d has bestowed upon me I settled on the title *Right Place, Right Time Part 2*.

And now begin my stories...

ANTI-SEMITISM: IT'S ALL AROUND US

Anti-Semitism is prejudice towards, or discrimination against, Jews. This sentiment is a form of racism, and a person who harbors it is called an anti-Semite. While reading the three following stories the reader may get the feeling that I experienced anti-Semitism directed toward me. I have many times and won't let ignorance affect my life, but I am very aware that it exists and is all around us.

Don't Call Me Doc Again—Bridge (1972)

When I was around seventeen years old a family friend with political contacts helped me land a summer job with the city of Providence, Rhode Island painting bridges. On the very first day I knew immediately that I had to keep my mouth shut and simply do what I was told. I showed up to the office garage at 7:00 a.m. sharp and was told to start loading the trucks with paint, brushes, buckets, and some scaffolding. While I struggled to load everything the ten or twelve city workers sat around, drank coffee, ate donuts, and read the paper. I asked numerous times when we would begin working and I was told to mind my own business. Around 9:00 a.m. everyone got into the three or so trucks and we headed out to the job. We were going to be scraping and painting the Point Street Bridge located near the East Side neighborhood of Providence, Rhode Island. This bridge carries Point Street from the jewelry district to Wickenden Street at the base of College Hill. When we arrived, the foreman told me to unload the trucks while the rest of the crew did nothing but smoke and bullshit. One of the workers, a guy named Tony, started giving me a bunch of crap and calling me "Doc" as he had heard that I was planning to go to college to get an education. He said he read it on my job application. He also saw that I was wearing a *Chai* necklace, which figures prominently in the Jewish culture and stands for the meaning of life. He asked if I was Jewish and when I said yes, he began to taunt me with racist, derogatory words and would continue off and on for the remainder of my summer employment. I approached the foreman and he replied that it was only a joke and I should get over it and get to work or he would write me up and suspend me without pay. Of course, later on that afternoon I called my family friend and he told me to just go back to work, do my job, and mind my own business.

I knew that sooner or later I would have to speak up and tell Tony to knock it off, but of course I was afraid. He was an uneducated, ignorant, anti-Semitic piece of shit and I knew he would taunt me and tease me whenever he could, which he did. He was always looking to start some shit with me and also directed me when and where to scrape, or paint, or empty the trucks of equipment and supplies. I think the foreman delighted in seeing me aggravated and probably was hoping I would quit. I refused to quit or be intimidated, but was always watchful when Tony came anywhere near me. The summer would go on and I would get into the usual routine of showing up for work at 7:00 a.m. and wait a few hours to get to the jobsite. Did I mention that the authorized lunch break was from 11:30 a.m. to 12:00 p.m. but the entire crew except for yours truly would mysteriously disappear and come back around 2:00 p.m. smelling like booze? While they were all gone, I took it upon myself to paint, scrape, or do anything that needed to be done. I wasn't going to sit around and do nothing so I always found something to do. When the foreman asked me if any city officials came by looking for any of the workers and I told him no, he then told me to stay just in case a supervisor came by to ask questions. If one did, I was to say that they had gone back to the office to get paint and supplies. To make sure that I got the point, the foreman would sometimes have one of the drivers drive to the end of the bridge, which was approximately eleven hundred feet long, and park the truck. Then sometime before the end of the day, he'd have me take some ladders and/or cans of paint back to the truck and load it. When I asked him why the truck couldn't be brought back to the opposite end to make it easier for me to load he would simply smile and say "because I said so." Once again, I did what I was told.

Sometimes I would think about throwing Tony off the bridge. The problem was there were too many witnesses, so I would think all day long about a way to aggravate Tony instead. One day towards the end of the summer Tony greeted with me with one of his favorite terms of endearment, which generally was either "Doc Jewboy" or "Doctor Jew." By this time, I'd had it with his bullshit. Every one of the crew would laugh except for one of the truck drivers. He would occasionally tell me that he never had an opportunity to further his education and that he was proud of me. He told me that if Tony ever started a fight with me or got too aggressive, he would help me get out of trouble.

Sure enough, around the last few days of summer the time came for me to exact my revenge. I was painting one of the top rails when I heard Tony call my name and that he wanted me to lower down a can of paint while he was dangling below the bridge. It was the perfect opportunity. I tied the can of paint very loosely and began to lower it. While out of eyeshot of anyone I shook the rope up and down and the can of paint fell and hit him in the head, knocking him off balance. He fell off the scaffolding around fifteen feet or so into the water. I immediately yelled for help and a few of the workers threw a rope down to him and pulled him to safety. Tony began to yell and swear at me and accused me of dropping the paint on his head on purpose. I vigorously denied doing this and the truck driver came over and told the foreman that he had seen Tony swinging back and forth. He believed that Tony wasn't exercising proper judgment and that was the reason why he fell off the scaffolding. I thanked the driver and shook his hand. Tony continued to berate me and said he would get back at me. Luckily for me I never saw Tony again.

As for the truck driver, whom I will call "Boo," would you believe what happened a few years later, after I had finished college? I was visiting a family friend who owned a scrap metal company in Providence off Route 95. When I went inside a rather large man came up to me and asked if I remembered him. When I said I couldn't recall he said he had a question to ask me. He said "Doc, do you remember Tony from the Point Street Bridge?" When I said yes, Boo said he was the truck driver from my summer job. He then said he saw me dangling the can of paint over Tony's head and that when it hit him it forced the scaffolding to sway, which was the actual reason Tony fell off. He told me that even though Tony could have been seriously hurt, he was proud of me for finishing my education and he respectfully would call me Doc anytime he would see me again. What's the moral of the story here? I guess you could say some heads are stronger than others. While I used mine for an education, Tony used his to attempt to balance a can of paint. Every time I go over the Point Street Bridge I think of Tony and the day his lights were put out, if only for a minute or so. As for Tony, I believe that he "painted" himself into a corner (pun intended). I wasn't going to take any more of his bullshit, then or ever.

Mission complete.

Sean O'Brien and Hitler Comments (1985 - 1987)

In 1985 I was employed by the Department of Defense in Boston, Massachusetts. I worked with many dedicated civil servants, some of whom were attorneys, accountants, engineers, and contracting specialists. One of my coworkers happened to be all three. For the sake of this story, I will call him Sean O'Brien. When I started my position, I was told by the director of my agency, who also happened to be Jewish, that this employee had a tendency to make many negative and derogatory comments about people of color as well as people of the Jewish faith. For some unknown reason he took an immediate dislike of me, perhaps since he felt that I was getting preferential treatment from the director. This was far from reality. On day one Mr. O'Brien was assigned as my supervisor. He called me into the office and was explaining some rules and procedures when he asked if I was Jewish. When I responded that I was he began to curse at me and went on to tell me that it was the fault of me and all of my ancestors that his family suffered during the Great Potato Famine in Ireland.

His went on to explain that his family was lucky to get sponsors to come to the United States and settled in the heavily populated Irish community of Boston, Mass where some of his relatives worked at low-level paying jobs in factories that happened to be owned by a Jewish family. He recounted stories from family members about their struggle, and since they all berated and despised Jews, he was continuing the family tradition.

I tried not to have much to do with him but he continued to be my supervisor for some time. We unfortunately traveled together numerous times, and I always kept our conversations related to the business at hand and never ever discussed personal issues with him. I always knew in my gut that we would have some type of falling out and within a few short years it happened.

I was attending a meeting in a federal building in Boston with numerous high-ranking civil servants along with Mr. O'Brien. After introductions all around he suddenly asked me and the agency director if we'd heard that Rudolf Hess had died. Hess was not only Adolph Hitler's deputy and party leader, he was a friend and confidant of Hitler and was sentenced to Spandau Prison in Berlin where he was the sole inmate. He died on August 17, 1987, apparently the victim of suicide, but for some unknown reason they said he was strangled. Either way I hope that he suffered greatly and rots in hell.

When I told Mr. O'Brien that Hess should have dropped dead many years prior, he replied "Do you know what your problem is?" When I said no, he replied "Hitler should have gassed you all." Without thinking, I calmly reached across the table, grabbed him by the tie, and smashed his head into the table. As he screamed in pain, blood came out of his mouth like a scene in a horror movie. The federal police in the building were alerted and came immediately, along with medical personnel. They read me my rights and placed me into custody, then took me down to process me for assault charges on a federal employee. At this time, I was allowed to make a phone call. I immediately contacted my uncle who was very friendly with Senator John H. Chafee who represented Rhode Island in the US Senate from 1976 to 1999. My uncle advised me to refrain from making any comments and told me that he would call the senator's office and I should be released from custody shortly.

As we all know the wheels of justice sometimes go round and round but that doesn't happen if someone political and powerful gets involved. Sure, enough, within half an hour or so I was released from the holding cell and was told to appear in a federal court in Boston the following week. As I was being let go, one of the police officers said to me that I must have friends high up and all I did was smirk on the way out. The next day or so I met my uncle and someone from the senator's office and was told that the charges against me were dismissed and that no court appearance would be needed. I was, however, told not to associate with my coworker again and he no longer would be my supervisor. Little did

I know at the time that some of the high-ranking guests at the meeting were also Jewish and were appalled at the behavior of my coworker. I also heard later that all the other witnesses at the table all stated that they didn't see anything. Mr. O'Brien hired an attorney to sue me and the agency and requested a copy of the videotape of the meeting. Since I worked in a building that required security clearance for all employees, everything in certain parts was videotaped. For some unknown reason, the tape of the meeting was mysteriously deleted in an error similar to the Watergate tape missing eighteen and a half minutes. Since there were no witnesses and no video all charges against me were expunged.

A few years later I put in for a transfer to another federal agency in Newport, Rhode Island. At my going-away party many of my coworkers attended to wish me success in my new endeavors. Would you believe that Mr. O'Brien, my former supervisor and continuing anti-Semite, also attended? I was concerned about what he would say to me but he was fairly cordial. He extended his hand and told me that he was glad to see me go. He told me that he felt because of the incident a few years back his career was derailed and he no longer was considered for higher management positions. He blamed me of course but when he directly asked me if I or any of my political friends had anything to do with hurting his career, I simply told him no, of course not. My parting words to him were as follows: "Mr. O'Brien, I need to excuse myself and get another large serving of potato salad, and I heard the potatoes came from Ireland, the land of your ancestors." I never saw or heard from him again.

Pool in Florida - I Jew'd Him Down (2001)

During the winter of 2001 my wife Barbara and I went to Florida to soak up the sunshine, go to flea markets, visit some friends, and see the alligators. I have always been fascinated by these creatures and we would always take an airboat ride in the Everglades when we visited.

One afternoon while relaxing at the pool in Fort Lauderdale we met a young guy, around thirty-five years of age, and we began to chat about the weather and where we hailed from. I told him that we were from Rhode Island, to which he immediately replied that we were Yankees and that he had heard that was where "all the Jews lived." I told him that didn't make any sense but I remained calm and civil as the beer-bellied ignorant son of a bitch continued to foam at the mouth while uttering other ignorant racist and homophobic comments. He told us that he was visiting from Michigan where everyone either worked in the automobile factories making cars or were unemployed. I am not sure where he got his data from but assumed since he was doing a lot of drinking, he must have got it out of his ass.

We tried to move away from him but he continued to spew his ignorance. You might ask why we didn't get out of the pool. We had every right to swim and relax as much as the asshole did. I tried to be calm and then he asked us if we had planned to go to any of the great flea markets nearby like the Swap Shop on Sunrise Boulevard. When we mentioned that we loved going there, he stated that when he would buy items he always "Jew'd" them down. Barbara politely and assertively told him we were Jewish and asked if he knew what that term meant. He replied that it meant to save money. Barbara told him that it was a derogatory phrase similar to "gypped" from the term "thieving Gypsies" or to flimflam someone. He, of course, didn't apologize to us. Instead, he asked us if we wanted to join him and his girlfriend later on for drinks. We politely declined and didn't see him for the rest of our vacation.

On the way out of the pool, the thought did cross my mind that I could go purchase an alligator and have it brought back to the hotel, and I could throw it in the pool when he alone was swimming. The only thing that stopped me from doing so was the cost to purchase and transport it. And of course, there was the problem of how to dispose of any of the man's remains after he was partial dinner for the alligator.

Since then, whenever I purchased a vehicle that was manufactured in Detroit, Michigan and it began to have issues, I would think back to the beer-guzzling, beer-bellied, ignorant, uneducated asshole anti-Semite. So instead, now I always buy a car made in Japan or South Korea, where cars are built primarily by robots and not stupid humans. "I'll drink to that!

AUTOMOBILE INCIDENTS

Handkerchief Story (1966)

I have told this story many times before. My family and friends have repeatedly told me that they are tired of hearing it but they always indulge me and let me tell it over and over again. I guess the real reason I enjoy this story is that it brings me back to the time I spent with my late father and how much he loved me and I loved him.

My dad was tall, handsome, charismatic, and always wore a suit or shirt and tie wherever he went. He was from the old school and he felt it was important to be polite and respectful of everyone and everything. He once told me that if you want to feel successful, then dress professionally. This attitude made him a successful person and businessman and even today, many years since his death at the age of forty, people will come up to me to tell me how nice my father was and how nice he dressed.

My dad always had a handkerchief (hanky) in his suit jacket pocket with his initial on it. Shortly before my eleventh birthday he surprised me with a three-pack of white hankies with the initial K in big bold lettering on them. I cherished those hankies as a most precious gift. I proudly would put them in my suit jacket pockets, or in a shirt pocket whenever the opportunity arose.

To this day many years later I put one of my monogrammed hankies in my suit jacket pockets and take them with me to use whenever I have an allergy issue or a cold or just to complete the outfit that I am wearing.

Now to get to the story. One summer day around 1966 we were on the way to our beach house. For some odd reason I had a bloody nose that day.

My dad told me to take the hanky out of my jacket and used it to stop the bleeding. I felt bad using it but it had to be done.

The bleeding stopped and I rolled it up in my hand, and without telling anyone I threw out the window. Boy was I upset with myself for doing such a stupid thing. My dad saw me and was very upset as well. We were going down Tower Hill Road and Dad turned the car around and went back up to the tower and back again so we could attempt to find the handkerchief. We never did that day. On the way home my dad told me he was punishing me for what I did and asked me how I could throw away one of my prized possessions, my hanky. I began to cry. I was embarrassed and ashamed at what I did but mostly I was upset that I lost a gift my father gave me. My dad died a few years later and I never forgot him or the hanky.

Around 1978, the year before I met Barbara, I happened to be driving to the beach and was traveling down Tower Hill Road. I don't know if I said a prayer about the hanky or not but out of the corner of my eye, I noticed something in a bush on the side of the road. I needed to go back up the street since there was no place to park except a driveway that led up to someone's home.

I approached the driveway and got a funny feeling in my mind and stomach that I would be able to find my hanky from years ago. I got out of my car and saw a small white piece of fabric. It was stuck in a large bush with spiky branches poking through. I carefully put my hand in and pulled on it and gasped. I saw a small remnant of the letter K from my hanky and realized how lucky I was to find one of my most prized possessions.

I laughed and cried at the same time and brought the remnant home with me. I kept it sealed in a plastic bag for many years until the cloth disintegrated.

I learned a few valuable lessons that day.

1. Littering is never the right or cool thing to do.
2. Treasure your most valuable possessions.

3. Keep your eyes and heart open because miracles do happen. One small miracle happened to me that day, and it was a connection to my father that was reestablished.

Here's to you Dad. I love you and miss you. And rest assured, I will never ever misplace my hankies with the letter K ever again.

Locking Keys in Station Wagon and Dad Was Mad (1966)

When I was around eleven years old or so my dad would take us to Monahan's Dock located in Narragansett, Rhode Island in the summer, many times to go fishing. This was a local fishing spot which was and still is very popular with everyone around.

My dad would pack up the car with the three boys or whoever happened to be behaving that week and we'd bring a lunch with us, and all our fishing equipment. Once in a while if we were too tired, our dad would let us wait inside the car which was a mere foot away from the dock.

He trusted us to stay in the car and let us keep the radio on. He would always tell us that when we were done, we were to shut off the radio and put the keys in one of our pockets, then shut the door and lock it. Remember, this was before automatic doors. There were just push-button locks. He would show us how to push the lock down and then shut the door tight, but always reminded us to take the keys with us.

One of these days my brother and I were in the car and we were fooling around throwing the keys back and forth; we didn't give it any thought. When we were done about twenty minutes later, we got out of the car and locked the doors. We went down the stairs to the pier and Dad asked us where the keys were. Oops. Obviously the looks on our faces let our dad know we did something wrong. We forgot to take the keys with us.

Remember this was in the days before AAA. My dad was furious. We had no cell phones and no way to call Mom who might have had a set of keys at home. The problem that day was that, even if we'd found a payphone to call our landline, my mother had taken my two sisters shopping in Wakefield, Rhode Island and wouldn't be home for several hours. Even though it was hot outside my dad told us we had to walk home. It was really only about a twenty-minute walk. The problem was "hot" meant it was about ninety-five degrees out and we were sweltering from the heat.

On the way home, even though I could see my dad was mad, he did not yell at us or chastise us. He decided to teach us a lesson about life and doing the right thing.

While walking my dad told stories about his childhood; how he did things that were wrong and how it had affected him and his entire family. I wasn't sure then if I even paid attention but I was very upset that my dad was upset. I began to cry and told my dad I was sorry and I apologized. He said it could have been much worse.

By the time we got home my mom had come back from shopping and we were pooped. We were going to go take a nap and relax. However, my dad said that wasn't going to happen as if he had to walk back in extreme heat to get the car then we were going to join him.

My two brothers refused and started yelling so my dad said they were grounded for the rest of the weekend and couldn't leave the house. When I heard them getting grounded and in trouble, in my head I basically went, *oops, I'm going to keep my mouth shut and tell my dad I'll be more than happy to walk back with him.*

On the way back my dad and I were chatting and he put me on his shoulders. I thought I was the king of the world. I wanted so bad to have my dad be proud of me and not be mad. He told me that there were two rules in life. Rule number one: Your parents are always right. Rule number two: Follow rule number one. I've learned that in family and in marriage.

Station Wagon Hit Broadside in Downtown Providence (1967)

In 1967 my dad, his father, and his brother owned the Philip Dwares Company in Pawtucket, Rhode Island. This company sold Chrysler automobiles.

My dad used to take the family out for rides. One day my dad came home with a brand-new station wagon that had wooden panels on the side.

Remember, back then there was no such thing as seatbelts, so he piled all his five children and my mom into the car.

We left our home in the East Side and headed downtown. We were on College Hill, approaching the intersection of South Main Street, when it happened.

Out of nowhere a car came barreling through the intersection and slammed us broadside.

The car went round and round for what seemed an eternity. After spinning five or six times we came to an abrupt halt. My mom was screaming and my dad had a pained look on his face.

Miraculously none of us were hurt. I guess since we were just crossing the intersection at a normal speed and the man was about to slow down before he hit us, none of us suffered any serious injuries.

We all got out of the car and waited for the police and ambulance to arrive. The man who hit us apologized and when the police arrived he admitted responsibility. Since none of us were really hurt, the EMTs checked us all out and told my parents that they should take us out for ice cream.

We were lucky that day and I remember thinking that my dad and mom were our real-life heroes. Besides being my parents, they did what parents are supposed to do. Even though they could not prevent the accident they did the best they could to protect us, get us checked out, and loved us. Ever since that day, anytime I get in a car I always make sure that my seatbelt is on and any passengers have theirs on as well.

DEATH AND OTHER HEALTH ISSUES

Dad Arrested After Finding Body at Narragansett Town Beach (1967)

In the summer of 1967, I was enjoying myself at our family beach house in Narragansett, Rhode Island with my two brothers and two sisters and my parents. On one of the hot and humid nights my dad would take a few of us down to the wall on Ocean Road and we would look out at the waves crashing on the rocks below. We always had a great time and he would tell us stories about his life and his adventures. He would also tell us that he could see China in the distance. One of his favorite things was telling us about the giant tuna that he would catch when he used his rod, the rod that he promised to someday give to me.

On one of these nights my older brother and I were walking along the seawall when my dad excitedly said that he saw what looked like a giant fish or whale popping up and down in the water below near the rocky shore. He told us to stay where we were as he went over the wall to see what it was. A minute or so later he yelled for us to back away from the wall. We listened and watched as he carried what looked to be a lifeless person from the water. He tugged and tugged and gradually was able to lift the man onto the sidewalk. He told my brother and I to run down to the local clam shack and have them call the police. Within a few minutes we heard sirens and they approached my dad, who at this point was carrying the man towards the police. When the police arrived, at first they weren't sure what was happening so they screamed at my dad and told him to gently put the man on the ground. They placed my dad under arrest until they figured out what was going on. Within a few minutes an ambulance arrived and when they realized that the man had drowned, they immediately released my dad from custody. My dad hugged us and told us that he was proud that we ran for help. He took us to Aunt Carrie's in Narragansett for a late-night snack. Within a day or so everyone in town knew that my dad was the man who attempted to help the man in the water, who had sadly already died. I will always remember the day and I have a "whale" of a fish story to tell for many years to come.

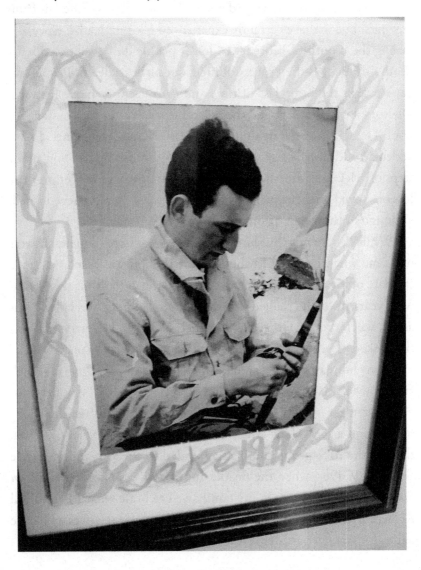

Family (Deaths, Births, and Anniversaries as of 2024)

Most families unfortunately experience painful episodes of death whether it be by sickness, depression, suicide, or natural causes. No one wants to admit it, but the day we are born begins the countdown to our ultimate destiny (demise). My family is no different from anyone's, but we have certainly experienced a lot of deaths, especially during the month of February. A lot of people don't want to discuss death. To me it is the process of life from birth to death. People can get stuck in the hourglass of time and can't seem to move forward. Doctors, social workers, and therapists like to discuss the five stages of grief: Denial, Anger, Bargaining, Depression, and Acceptance. I have added an additional stage, which I call Bullshit. No matter how many steps of grief there are, the one constant is that you never get over the loss of a loved one. The pain lasts and lingers. It's simply a new normal, although nothing ever again is truly back to normal.

While I am telling this short story I also want to tell you my answers one time when I was asked about my birthday. I was asked what was the date of my birth, to which I replied October 28. I was then asked what year, to which I replied Every Year. In the same conversation I was asked, when did my father die, to which I replied, February 19. I was then asked what year did he die, to which I replied, only once.

Many holidays are observed during the month of February—Black History Month, Humpback Whale Awareness Month, National Cancer Prevention Month, American Heart Month, and Valentine's Day to mention a few. Many Americans also celebrate February 7, 1964, the day the rock group the Beatles landed in the US, and of course February 9, 1964 when the Beatles appeared live on *The Ed Sullivan Show* for the first time. In my family we celebrate what I like to call Remembrance Day for all the family members and relatives who have left us for greener pastures (Death).

My dad died on February 19, 1968 at the age of forty after first being in a car accident and a few days later succumbing to a brain hemorrhage.

My dad's brother committed suicide on February 26, 1968, the day my father's shiva began (a shiva is seven-day period of mourning by immediate family after a member of the Jewish faith passes).

The week after my uncle died, still in 1968, one of my grandmother's closest relatives passed away as well.

I was the first person that I ever knew that went to three funerals in a row for beloved family members. I was out of school for three weeks straight. Do you think it affected my life, attitude, and actions? You bet your sweet ass it did. For many years after, my mom and my aunt's family *and* my uncle's family thought I was a potential suicide waiting to happen. They told me many years later the reason they thought I could take my own life was that I was a sensitive personality and always kept my thoughts to myself. I was lucky that I was smart enough to pull myself up from the depths of hell to become the man that I am today. I credit my wife Barbara Gold Dwares for being my anchor and keeping me on the straight and narrow road of life.

Let's move forward and then end with this.

Many years later my first cousin committed suicide. I never knew the actual reason, but family members told me depression and the loss of a parent were the main culprits.

My own son Max passed away at the age of twenty on February 18, 2004 due to complications related to his battle with leukemia. Max's funeral was on February 19, 2004, thirty-six years after the date my father died, February 19, 1968. Who could have possibly predicted that would happen?

And to top it all off my, older brother Neal passed away on February 11, 2024 at the age of sixty-nine.

Through all of these deaths in my family I have come to realize that Life is for the Living, it's not for the deceased. We are all here on the planet simply to leave the world a better place for those left behind. Death isn't something that shouldn't be talked about. It should be always talked about since it is also part of the process of life. To keep it bottled up inside is a guarantee for stress, tension, and aggravation for those left behind. I wish you all health, happiness, and above all a good Life.

HOSPITAL

The Nurse and Gun in Mouth (1980)

A cousin of mine was a nurse for many years. I can't and won't get into all the specifics of the story but so you all know it's the truth and nothing but the truth so help me G-d.

Disclaimer: Don't ever do what I did in the following story. It was reckless, immature, foolish and stupid, and could have resulted in me ending up in prison or worse.

My cousin was in the hospital working as a senior nurse and thoroughly enjoyed her work. She had then and still to this day has a heart of gold. She is loyal, compassionate, and is an overall wonderful human being. I am proud of her and all of her life's accomplishments. I had a deep admiration for her and still do.

One day she told me that a handsome young doctor asked her out on a date but she didn't feel he was right for her. She told me that he was arrogant and full of himself and wasn't nice to her or anyone else at work. He kept teasing her and asking her out on a date and finally one day said that he would ruin her career if she did not go to dinner with him. She was extremely upset.

I told her to tell him the next day at work to leave her alone and quit pestering her. At this stage he got very mean and nasty to her. I mentioned this story a few days later to my older brother, who said he would talk to a few of his friends and come up with a plan to have this guy stop bothering our cousin.

A few days later he called me, and told me to tell our cousin to tell the doctor she would go out with him on a date, but only if she could decide the time, the day, and the location.

They picked a Saturday night about 6:00 p.m. to go for a drive to

Swan Point Cemetery off Blackstone Boulevard in Providence, Rhode Island.

She told him that she liked taking rides to the cemetery because it made her feel calm.

On the night in question, we told her to be around a certain street in the cemetery at around 6:30 p.m. We also told her not to tell the guy anything, not to acknowledge that she knew any of us, and to stay in the car when we arrived at the location.

At the given time, myself, my brother, and his friend who happened to be an off-duty police officer arrived in the cemetery and we immediately found the doctor's car at the designated spot.

My cousin had given us the make, model, and license plate.

My brother's friend pulled his car directly in back of the doctor's car and started beeping the horn and flashing the lights. A few seconds later the door opened up and a handsome, tall, well-dressed man, obviously the doctor, exited the car and started saying who the hell do we think we are beeping the horn in back of him.

Well in the next ten seconds my brother and the policeman open up their jacket pockets and took out what appeared to be .38 caliber pistols.

At this stage the doctor looked petrified. He said he was sorry he yelled and swore at us and that he would be on his way.

Well, it was too late for that. The off-duty policeman went up to the guy quickly and flashed his badge. He grabbed the guy by the collar and slammed him down on the hood while my brother put handcuffs behind his back.

The man immediately soiled his pants (in layman's terms he pissed himself) and cried like a baby.

Since the doctor did not know my brother, myself, or the off-duty policeman he was petrified.

We asked the doctor who was the young lady with him in the car and he said it was a friend of his who was a nurse. We told her to get out of the car and she did not acknowledge that she knew us. She said that this guy was bothering her and she tried to not go out with him but he insisted.

Wow. At this stage the doctor knew he was in big trouble.

The policeman took the man's wallet out and wrote down his name, address, date of birth, social security number, and credit card information.

When the doctor said that was illegal the policeman then did something even more illegal: he put the gun in the man's mouth and cocked the trigger. I didn't realize at the time but he had already taken the bullets out of the gun by the time he arrived at the scene. The man wailed like a baby and told us that he would never bother his date again. He understood we knew where he lived and he would end up getting a beating in the future if he bothered her again.

We told our cousin to get in the back of our car and she obliged and we left the scene. She was afraid to go to work the next day but I told her the doctor would not be bothering her again because he was petrified.

When she went to work a few days later she told me that the doctor had not shown up for work in the last few days. She asked the hospital staff members where the doctor was. They told her that the doctor for some unknown reason resigned his position and moved back to Dallas, Texas where he was from.

Do you think my cousin ever heard from him again? Do you think the man called the police on us or do you think the man disappeared? As of many years later as I write this story, my cousin has never heard from him again.

Well, I would like to say I'm happy this man never bothered her again, but I would also say there could have been a different way to resolve these issues. But at the time my brother decided to take the matter into his own hands and I stupidly went along for the ride.

My cousin never spoke about this again but was thankful that her relatives helped her.

I regret being involved in this incident and I'm sorry. However, sometimes when a cousin that you love is bothered or hurt, relatives will come to their defense.

The moral of the story is to think before you act. Sometimes rash decisions could end up being deadly; thankfully it didn't happen on this occasion.

Kevin Having Thyroid Surgery. Barbara Looking for Dog (2005)

Back in 2005 I had my thyroid removed when a small cancerous tumor was found after I had a car accident with my younger son, Jake. I went to my doctor a few days later and at first, he didn't see anything wrong. I kept complaining and he finally sent me for an MRI which determined that I had a herniated disc and a thyroid issue. A day or so later I was scheduled for a fine needle biopsy, which is when they stick a large needle in your neck to get a sample of the thyroid gland and the tissue is sent to the lab to get analyzed. A week or two went by and it was determined that I had a cancerous tumor in my thyroid which needed to be removed as the nodule was encapsulated, meaning it remained in place and hadn't spread to any other organs in my body.

I told the endocrinologist that I wanted to get a few other opinions and he suggested two radiologists who happen to be our friends. They both agreed that the thyroid should be removed immediately. I asked what were the possible complications. All three replied that the main issue was if the cancer spread; if I had the operation I would probably gain fifty pounds, which I did. I will also for the rest of my life take a synthetic thyroid medication called Synthroid.

Surgery was performed in 2005 to have my thyroid totally removed. I was given the option to only remove part of the thyroid where the cancer was, but was advised to remove the complete organ to be safe. All went well. While I was in the recovery room the day of my surgery Barbara told me that she and Jake went to look for a dog like a King

Charles Cavalier, which is kind of like a cocker spaniel. To this day I don't recall ever having a conversation about this, but they both claimed that I agreed to getting another animal. Of course, I was sedated so I didn't realize what they were talking about, but it was too late. A day or so later they came home with a dog who we called Ozzie who lived us until he passed away at the age of twelve in October 2017, a few days before we moved to our new ranch house in Garden City, Cranston.

Ozzie was a good dog. He was lovable, friendly, and had a unique personality of his own. He was a great pet and walking partner as well.

I guess you could say having a pet is good but then I would also say don't make any decisions or agreements while recuperating from surgery because you may be surprised with a new addition to your family.

As for my thyroid surgery, all went well in 2005. It's been almost twenty years and I've had no lasting issues.

Thank you for reading my short story, and all I can say is "woof" to you all.

Telephone in Pre-Operating Room During (2007) Disk Surgery

In the spring of 2007, I was in Miriam Hospital located in Providence, Rhode Island to repair a cervical disk in my neck that was injured during an automobile accident the year before when a driver lost control sliding on ice and slammed into my car. I won't get into the details but suffice to say it wasn't the most pleasant procedure, before, during, or afterwards. My wife Barbara came into the hospital with me and after providing my health insurance and other required documentation she was allowed to accompany me to the pre-op suite where I changed from my street clothes to a hospital gown and gave her my wallet and cell phone. After exchanging a few words, she left the room and told me she would stay in the hospital until my procedure was completed. A short time later a nurse came in and began the process of inserting an

IV and some meds to calm down my nerves. My doctor arrived shortly afterward, explained the procedure again, and said he would return soon. He then shut the curtain and told me to relax. Easy for him to say when I was the one on the table! I did think of getting up and escaping but I knew if I did then I would have to come back another day to begin the process over again.

About ten minutes later I heard a nurse calling out my name and when I said I was behind door number 3, I also jokingly asked if this was the *Let's Make a Deal* television show. She casually said that I had a telephone call and proceeded to hand me a telephone accompanied by a twenty-foot cord. She said that it must be somewhat important since only doctors and nurses could use a telephone in the operating area.

I realized that it couldn't have been Barbara since we had said "goodbye" or "see you later" a short time ago and she had my cell phone. I was getting a little groggy so when I answered the phone I said something like "Who the hell is this?" At the other end was my longtime friend Richard "Ricky" Levenson. He had seen a list of the patients who were having procedures that day and saw my name. Ricky is a unified communications engineer for Lifespan Corporate Services and handles all the IT and telecommunications issues for the Lifespan umbrella of hospitals. Ricky asked how I was doing and if I needed anything at the moment. When I asked could he help me escape before my procedure he simply said "Not a chance." When I asked him to get me a Diet Coke and some of my favorite chocolate covered cherries he again said no, but thanked me for telling him since he was getting hungry. In a few minutes or so he told me that he would call Barbara and he would check in on me later that day (which he did). We said our goodbyes and I told the nurse to come take the phone back. She asked me who I just talked to and when I said Ricky Levenson, she said that he was the most professional and friendly engineer that worked for Lifespan. I wholeheartedly agree. Even though we don't see each other as often as I would like, we always exchange pleasantries every time we meet and he always jokes about the time I answered the telephone in

the pre-op room years ago. And of course, I always remind him of the Diet Coke and the chocolate covered cherries. Maybe after he reads this story when my book is published, he will send me a case of Diet Coke and a box of the chocolate cherries since I probably have made him somewhat famous.

LESSONS IN LIFE

Bomb Under the Car (1976)

When I was close to twenty-one years old, I was attending Rhode Island College working to attain my bachelor's degree in psychology. Rather than continuing dorm life as I did at Roger Williams University, I moved into an apartment with my older brother and another friend. We lived in the Moshassuck Square Apartments located on Charles Street in Providence, Rhode Island.

I did fairly well in school and was on the dean's list my entire time in college, including when I returned later on to get a bachelor's degree in accounting from Johnson and Wales University.

While roommates with my older brother and one of his friends, they were always getting into some type of mischief. I knew sooner or later that they would do something that would get them in serious trouble.

My family was friendly with a detective who stayed in touch with my mother over the years to keep watch on us. At one point when my brother was in trouble again, the police friend decided to scare the crap out of us, which he did, at least to me. One late afternoon he came knocking on our apartment door and asked us to take a ride with him.

My brother got in the front seat and myself and the roommate got in back. Trying to impress us, he put the siren on, blasted the horn, and drove through every red light and stop sign until we got to the location of what he wanted to show us. We got out of the police car and we then approached a car that was completely sealed around with yellow caution tape. He told us to walk underneath the tape towards the car, which we did because at the time we thought this was cool, almost like a *Miami Vice* episode from the 1980s. As we approached, we were told to look underneath the car, and to my amazement I saw between six and ten sticks of dynamite with some blasting caps attached to the engine. The detective explained that the man who was supposed to be driving the car was meant to be blown to smithereens when the car started, but by luck or fate the man heard a strange noise and realized in a hurry that he needed to get out and call the police. Someone rigged the car to blow up and it was sheer luck that bomb failed to explode, thereby saving the man's life. I'll tell you what; this made a drastic impression on me, but my brother and his friend still ran wild for many years to come. After that day I decided to complete my education and lead a straight and narrow life. This wasn't the movies. This was reality and I didn't like it. The incident taught me to take the right path in life, to not get involved with any illegal stuff or hang out with the wrong people.

That day I was given an offer I couldn't refuse to stay away from evil and bad people. I have always done so and I'm happy for that.

To end this short story, I will be candid here and tell you the conclusion of the life of my brother and his friend. Both of them went on to get in various types of trouble later on in life through bad marriages, trouble with the police, and a few other incidents that I can't share with the reader. The roommate passed away from a heart attack at the age of sixty-four on Christmas day in 2019 and my brother passed away from a heart attack at the age of sixty-nine on February 11, 2024. I always wonder if it had been due to the life they lived or simply health issues. Only G-d himself knows the answer.

Know the correct street in Brooklyn, New York (1979)

I met Barbara Gold on March 11, 1979 and she would become my wife on June 29, 1980 nearly eighteen months later. Barbara had just returned from living in Israel for a year teaching immigrant children in a development town known as Dimona. Sometime after we met, her friend Ann Kutner, now known as Ann Greenstein, invited us both to come to Brooklyn and stay with her mother Mildred Kutner. Ann and Barbara had met in the same program in Israel and become good friends as they still are many years later. We drove to New York for a long weekend and arrived in Brooklyn on Avenue T and East Twenty-Second Street where all the houses were attached and all looked alike. One of the first things that I noticed was it was nearly impossible to find a parking space nearby and residents and guests would drive around the block numerous times to find a space near their home. We soon found a place to park and I nervously and shyly met Ann and her mother Mildred. Both Ann and her mom immediately made me feel comfortable and we settled in for a nice enjoyable weekend.

On Sunday morning I told Mildred (she told me to feel comfortable calling her by her first name) that I would find a bagel shop and get bagels, cream cheese, whitefish, and lox for a late brunch to thank her for letting us stay for the weekend. When I asked her to direct me to the local place she laughed and said that every block had many bagel shops. Remember, this was a time before cell phones and GPS so I got into the car and drove until I found a shop. After a few minutes of driving, I found the shop, went in, and ordered everything that we would all like, and included some pastry and pickles as well. I thought all those New Yorkers spoke funny but in reality, it was probably me. As I am accustomed to chatting with anyone (my twelve-year-old granddaughter Maya tells me I will even talk to a shoe) I lost track of time and also of the address I was supposed to return to. I got back in my car and headed back to Avenue T and East Thirty-Second Street.

I took the bags of food out of the car and ran up the stairs to the house as if I was a conquering hero returning from battle. I rang the doorbell and an unfamiliar face came to the door and asked me what I was doing there. Since I didn't know any of the Kutners' friends or relatives I began to walk forward into the house when the man at the door told me to stop and was happy to unbutton his sport jacket and showed me a police badge and a GUN. At first, I thought he was joking, but in a matter of a minute or two I realized he wasn't. He asked me who I was, where I lived, and who I was looking for and what address. He soon realized that I was lost. I eagerly told him of the Kutners' at East Twenty-Second Street. He laughed out loud. He invited me in and there were ten to fifteen people in the house enjoying bowlfuls of pasta, sausages, meatballs, etc. He told me to sit down as his wife filled up my plate and I told them all the story of me being lost.

Anthony Rosario Persico (at least that's the name I remember) the police officer got on the phone and called the station house and in a matter of minutes he found out where the Kutners lived and got them on the telephone. He explained to Mildred that I would be staying for brunch and I would get a police escort home in a few hours. When I told him that there was food in my car, he told me to bring it inside and he kept it in the fridge until I was done eating. We all sat along the table and I was introduced to Anthony's wife Carmella and many Tonys, Marias, Biancas, and Isabellas. We ate, laughed, and they told many stories of them growing up in Brooklyn and I told a few about my life as well.

After brunch I politely explained that I needed to get my food out of the fridge and bring it back to the home that I was staying in for

the weekend. Anthony asked me if I wanted a police escort back and I obliged him and said yes but only if the sirens could be blasting and we could go through some red lights and stop signs. I thanked everyone for their hospitality and I walked to my car as we waited for a few police vehicles to arrive. Within minutes I was motioned to get in my car and get behind the police car in front and Anthony and his police car would be in back. The sirens began to blare and speed along the street and we arrived at my destination in about ten minutes. As we got in front, the police cars continued to blast their horns and sirens until Barbara, Ann, and Mildred came out to greet the returning hero who had mastered the art of twirling pasta with a spoon and a fork. I continued to tell this story for many years to come and always laugh as I thoroughly enjoyed my day. It was a scene reminiscent of Clemenza teaching Michael to make meatballs and pasta in the Godfather movies or a scene in *The Sopranos*. "Now youse know the real story."

Woman on Train (1990)

While employed by the US Department of Defense Logistics Agency in Boston, Mass during the years of 1985 to 1991, most of the time I commuted by train from Attleboro, Mass to South Station, located in downtown Boston. I generally took the 5:40 a.m. train which would arrive at 6:40 a.m. giving me enough time to walk to my workplace, the Federal building at 495 Summer Street. I usually worked from 7:00 a.m. to 3:30 p.m. On one of these occasions, I learned a valuable lesson in life. This lesson taught me to be humble, and keep my mouth shut. I can't remember the exact date but the incident is emblazoned into my mind and I will never repeat it.

The train was moving through the normal corridor and made its usual stops along the way. Sometime around 6:20 a.m. or so I noticed that my watch had stopped ticking, even though Timex brands had a reputation that they could take a licking but always keep ticking. I politely asked the fellow passenger next to me for the time, but at first, she didn't respond. She was busy drinking her coffee and reading the newspaper. I asked her again, and again I received no response. This time I (ignorantly) turned to her and asked if she was deaf. Still no response.

I then tapped her on the shoulder and looked in her eyes and when I next spoke, she said that she was mostly deaf but could read my lips. She then began to touch her ears and adjust her hearing aids. She chastised me and said that I was impolite, rude, and ignorant as she said that she wasn't totally deaf and could get the gist of my insensitive comments. I immediately said that I was sorry and tried to explain that my watch had stopped working. She said that was no excuse for my rude behavior. I apologized profusely and asked if I could buy her a coffee and muffin when we arrived at the station as a sign of my acceptance of my bad behavior. She initially said yes.

While getting off the train I noticed she appeared to be pregnant so I asked her how far along she was and she got a very sad look on her face while tears rolled down her cheeks. She said that she wasn't having a baby and instead had a large cancerous tumor that would have to be operated on in the next few weeks after she was done with her numerous chemotherapy and radiation treatments. Once again, I realized that I had put my foot in my mouth. This time she said that she wouldn't accept a coffee and muffin and that she hoped she would never meet me or anyone else like me ever again. I tried to apologize again and she wouldn't accept it. We parted ways and I thought about the incident for many days and vowed to never again repeat it, which I have not.

What Max Gold Dwares Wrote About His Jewish Faith While Battling Cancer (2001)

As it says in Bereshit (meaning the beginning or the first word in the first weekly Torah portion in the annual Jewish cycle of the Torah reading), the Torah is the law or teaching of Judaism. "In the beginning G-d created the heaven and the earth... And G-d created man in his own image... And G-d blessed them." A path diverges to two in the woods. The one more frequently traveled leads to a life of godlessness, squander, and misery. The other leads to a life of study, religion, Torah, and G-d. I took the path less traveled and moved onwards toward G-d. I was made in the image of G-d and he blessed me. That would have been enough, but then he gave me the Ten Commandments. That would have been enough, and yet he gave me the Torah. Because of this immense generosity I feel vast unending adoration, and eagerness to serve G-d. Because of both my love and devotion to G-d I am deeply committed to my Judaism and that of others.

Due to my deep devotion to Judaism, I was more inclined to overcome tremendous obstacles, as well as maintain my faith during my tribulations. Since the discovery of my cancer not once did I have to grapple with my faith. Not once did I ask "Why me?" nor did I question G-d. I just accepted my situation as reality, began dealing with it and proceeded to go on with my life. I have found that one can find strength from three main sources: Strength from others, from myself, and ultimately from faith in G-d. My faith and ultimately my strength to go on has come from my devotion to Judaism. I found this in the Book of Job. The focus of this story is that Job was smitten "with sore boils from the sole of his foot even unto his crown." (Job 3:7) and yet through it all, through the disease, through the death of his family and destruction of his property all John can say of G-d is that "Though He slay me, yet will I trust in Him" (Job 13:15). When I found out about my diagnosis one of the first things I thought of was the story of Job and how he dealt with his grief. This little-known book of the Holy Scriptures was truly an inspiration to me and has helped me deal with my grief and maintain my faith.

Recently I have started upon a number of unique endeavors, such as striving to become a Rabbi, as well as beginning a book on faith. I undertook these tasks to reaffirm my faith as well as bring faith to others. Judaism has been, is, and will always be my inspiration. The history, the culture, the religion itself all have contributed to my devotion and commitment to Judaism. I want to bring my love, my faith, my inspiration, my Judaism to others; I feel that with my knowledge of Judaism, and with the tragedies I have endured I will be able to help others with my words. My book will deal primarily on faith in G-d and how it can help one deal with their pain. After college I will attend the Jewish Theological Seminary of America. With the knowledge I attain there I will become a student of the Rabbinate, a Rabbi. I feel that with my current knowledge, in addition to what I will learn there, coupled with my unique experiences, I will truly be able to help people. Not just physically and mentally, but also with and through faith.

A main aspect of Judaism is Tzedakah, and one of my primary goals in life has been working towards the betterment of the lives of others. Rabbi Schneerson once said "If you see what needs to be repaired and how to repair it, then you have found a piece of the world that G-d has left for you to complete." I have always maintained my commitment to finding my piece of the world to complete. Throughout my life I have helped those less fortunate than myself an uncountable number of times. In the Decembers of 1999 and 2000 I traveled with my high school Harry Elkin Midrasha Community High School to Philadelphia to work with the Trevor's Place Project to help the homeless. We traveled throughout the city bringing food, clothing, and blankets to men, women, and children living on the streets. Three times (in March 1999, February 2000, and February 2001) I again traveled with my high school, this time to Washington, D.C., in order to learn more ways for me to help others less fortunate than myself. While learning to help others, I helped them at the same time. On two of my visits, I helped to refurbish a community center, and on the third visit I was able to see the fully completed fruits of my labor. I have completed a number of other projects, from volunteering at a homeless shelter in Warwick, to organizing food and clothing drives at my school. But the project that I did, that made me feel as though I have made the most difference was making sandwiches. Recently I spearheaded a project with a few of my friends to make peanut butter and jelly sandwiches. So far, we have fed more than five hundred people through our work with Travelers Aid.

I am profoundly committed to my Judaism and that of others because of both my love and devotion to G-d. My faith in G-d has helped guide me throughout my life. God has given me direction; G-d has given me a purpose in life. When faced with a seemingly insurmountable problem, my commitment to Judaism, and my faith G-d provided me with a means to overcome my leukemia. One way in which I demonstrate my faith to G-d is by performing many different acts of Tzedakah from feeding to clothing others. In addition, I have also aspired to bring my faith to others. I am doing this primarily in two ways. First, I am currently writing a book on how faith can provide one with the strength to overcome seemingly impossible obstacles. Second, I will become a Rabbi. Through this and my book I hope to be able to bring my faith in G-d and commitment to Judaism to others.

Written by my son, the late Max Gold Dwares sometime around March 2001 after his diagnosis with leukemia. May he rest in peace and may his memory *always* be a blessing.

"While reading the above from one of Max's scrapbooks, I realized that Max had a much deeper insight to life than I and many others could ever possibly comprehend. I wondered while reading, in between me crying, if I ever could or did become half the man that Max was even when he passed away at the young age of twenty." Written by Kevin Dwares on Thursday, March 28, 2024.

French Drains (2024)

What are French drains and why are they used? A French drain is a trench filled with a perforated pipe and gravel that allows water to drain naturally from your basement out to your yard away from your home. They are used primarily when water seeps into a basement but have many other uses in construction and landscaping. The following story is true and the best advice I would give is buyer beware.

During the heavy rainy season in Rhode Island beginning in December 2023, many homeowners experienced rain like never before. Alot of people's basements were flooded; mine just had a small amount of water weeping through where the wall meets the floor. We were told by numerous professionals that this is called "hydrostatic pressure," where the rain saturates the ground until the water has nowhere to go but up, resulting in flooded basements. After consulting with numerous friends of mine who are plumbers, it was advised that we invest in French drains to hopefully eliminate the water in the basement and prevent flooding from happening again.

Early in March 2024 I began to get estimates and proposals from various companies that would install French drains. The companies that I inquired of were small, medium, and large in size and all had many years of experience. One of the things that all of them told me, besides that the work needed to be done, was that they all required a 50 percent down payment. The reason behind this was a lot of them had contracts with homeowners and had the work done and never got paid. I didn't like this idea about down payments but I needed the work to be done. First thing I did was review all the proposals and make a decision as to who was the best fit for my project. After I narrowed it down to a few I went to the Rhode Island contractor review board to get copies of the insurance policies that were currently in place. These were necessary in case the contractor damaged anything or something happened to him or his employees. I selected a company which had been in business in Rhode Island for over forty years with a good reputation, or so I thought.

Reluctantly I gave the contractor a down payment on March 14, 2024 and we settled on Monday, March 25, 2024 and Tuesday, March 26, 2024 to do the work. He promised me they would take a day and a half or two days maximum.

I gave the down payment using my credit card even though it could have ended up adding an additional 5 percent to the final cost of the project.

Almost immediately the next day he called to tell me he needed to reschedule our project due to scheduling conflicts. He then rescheduled us for Thursday, March 28, 2024 and Friday, March 29, 2024. Remember, during this time we were having rain off and on (and on, and on, and on) and some of it was getting in the basement.

The day before he was to begin work, he called me once again and said he had a big job with the city and he would not be able to do my work in the revised time frame that he promised me. After that day his office manager called and told me they rescheduled for Wednesday, April 3, 2024 and Thursday, April 4, 2024. The company owner personally got on the phone and promised he'd be coming back on April 3, 2024 and spend that day and the next completing the entire project. At approximately 9:30 a.m. on the promised date, the company president showed up at our house with two other people, his son and another coworker, to being jackhammering the basement.

The owner left shortly after 10:30 a.m. and his son stayed until 1:00 p.m. The other employee stayed until approximately 2:00 p.m. He told me they would be returning on Thursday.

On Thursday morning April 4, 2024 I received a call from the owner saying that his employees all called in sick that day and they would not be doing any work. He said he had to go back to working on a job for the city on Friday April 5, 2024 and promised 100 percent that they would come back to my house on Saturday April 6, 2024 to work on the project.

RIGHT PLACE, RIGHT TIME

On Saturday morning April 6, 2024 I was in touch with the company owner many times and he said the work could be done that day. No one showed up at our house, not even after we sent numerous text messages and calls to the owner's and his son's cell phones and to the company answering service throughout the day. They never responded and we never received any further messages via text, email, or cell phone. Meanwhile it rained again, and more water leaked into my basement.

Sometime later on Saturday I got a call from the company president and he promised that the work would be done on Sunday, April 7, 2024. I told him that we had to cancel a preplanned one-week vacation to Ogunquit, Maine so we wouldn't lose any money, to which he replied we could go on vacation any time. I told him that his workers needed to be at my house immediately to do more work. On Sunday morning no one showed up again so I contacted the company and told them their services were no longer required and I would be looking for another company to finish what they hadn't.

Meanwhile the company president told me that he left very expensive jackhammers and tools in my basement and he wanted them returned immediately. I told him that I would be sending him a letter and he would need to sign it for me to return the equipment. He said that no one would sign it. I told him that if someone didn't sign the letter, I would not return his equipment. Later that Sunday we called numerous other companies to come over and give us estimates because the work had to be done. One of those companies was a well-known one that could do the work within the next few days, but it would cost an additional $2,000. I had to give him 50 percent as a down payment to begin and the remaining 50 percent would be given at the conclusion of the project.

On Monday, April 8, 2024 I got a call from the president of the company whose services we'd terminated. He said the equipment needed to be returned immediately since he rented it from Taylor Rental and he demanded we do so. I told him that he could come to my house that day and pick up the equipment but only if a company representative signed for it.

On Tuesday morning April 9, 2024 the new company arrived at our house with three employees and immediately began to work on the basement. A short time later John the manager came to deliver bags of cement and put them in our garage. He came into the basement and immediately began to help the other employees work. The whole process with the new company was flawless. It was a coordinated effort with each person acting in synchronized fashion doing step-by-step what needed to be done. They first finished jackhammering the floor and cleaning out the trenches. The next thing they did was bring bags and bags of stone, perforated piping, and what appeared to be landscape fabric. The best type of fabric for a drainage project such as a drain field or French drain is non-woven geotextile landscape fabric. If your project requires high strength and also good drainage, then a high-end combination woven fabric could be suitable. The three employees worked at the project till around 4:30 p.m. or 4:45 p.m. By the time they left our house they were sweaty and exhausted from putting in a full day. They promised to return bright and early the next day.

As promised on Wednesday, April 10, 2024, four employees came to our home first thing in the morning. The manager informed us that he guaranteed the work would be done by the end of the day no matter what time that was. The first thing we did was put the fabric paper in the fifty-foot trench that stretched from the front of the foundation to both sides of the floor. Then they put down the crushed stone. Then they put down the perforated piping facing holes down, which allows the water that seeps up from the ground to get in the pipe and direct it towards the sump pump to be pumped out of the house. After that they wrapped the corrugated piping in the fabric. They then put more crushed stones on top of that. The crushed stone is used to allow the water to freely travel in the trench pit to get to the sump pit to have it pumped out of the house.

If you think that's all they did you're mistaken. The manager spent approximately three and a half more hours to pour cement on top of everything that they had dug up, leaving a nice smooth finish. The most difficult time they had was behind the heating system which is no more than two feet from the wall. I felt bad for the employees. While the cementing was going on, two technicians were working on installing a sump pump and getting it set up. They then put the sump pump cover on and bolted the whole unit to the floor and wall for support. After the work was done for the day, the manager said he would be back Friday morning around 9:00 a.m. to mop up all the dust and dirt on the floor. I laughed and said "Yeah don't forget to also come back with a vacuum cleaner."

On Thursday, April 11, 2024 Barbara and I dusted off everything that was on the shelves so we could put it back where it belonged. We were advised to wait a few more days until the cement was dry before we put everything back on the shelves and the floor.

Friday, April 12, 2024 at about 9:00 a.m. an employee came from the company to check everything and to make sure that we were totally satisfied with the project and the work they performed. While he was here, I had him drill two holes in the sump pump cover. One hole was for the dehumidifier to drain into the pit and the other was so I would be able to peek in with a flashlight to see if any water was in the pump. This was for my peace of mind, to let me know that the project was a success and the water was going to the sump pump pit where it was supposed to. He then went to his truck and came back with the mop and broom to take care of the floor. I asked him why he was doing that and he said "I told you on Wednesday I would be back to mop up the floor to make sure it was neat." I was quite impressed.

On Sunday, April 14 we put everything back on the shelves where it needed to be. One of the most important parts here was putting back the litter box for our cat Gaby since it had been upstairs in the hallway for the last week. It caused a definite improvement in Gaby's attitude; she was less nervous now that her food and litter box were back in the same location they'd always been.

This ended a very stressful two- to three-week period in our life from when we first got water in the basement, to the first contractor who failed to complete their obligations, to the second, professional, contractor I ended up dealing with to finish the project who thankfully satisfied the terms and conditions promised in our contract.

Even though we would have hoped we never had to have French drains installed on a house it was a necessary evil; but the unnecessary stress caused by the first contractor who did not complete the work exacerbated everything. I would not recommend anyone do this unless it's absolutely necessary; however, the few days or so that the work takes to be accomplished is more than worth the pain of having the water seep into your house continuously.

The only advice I can give you is I hope you get a reputable contractor to work in your house. We checked insurance, references, the contractor review board, and spoke to people who had dealt with the first company, and everything seemed to be fine. Now the project's over and while it wasn't as bad as Moses parting the sea when the Israelites were escaping from Egypt, it was bad for the family and very frustrating. All I can say is I'll drink to that.

Finally, as I mentioned in the beginning of my story, I put the down payment for the first contractor on my credit card. This allowed me to dispute the charge. After a month or so during which I had to submit a lot of documentation my credit card was fully credited 100 percent for what I paid the first contractor.

Lost and Found (Saint Anthony's Prayer)

As many of you know I have an uncanny knack for finding lost items such as wallets, keys, money, and many others. The following short stories illustrate that it never hurts to be in the right place at the right time.

Some of the readers may have no idea as to the who and what of Saint Anthony's prayer. Being of the Jewish faith I also had no idea so I did a small amount of research on him. To tell the truth I have myself said a prayer to him and have found numerous lost items as well.

RIGHT PLACE, RIGHT TIME

Saint Anthony of Padua is one of the Catholic Church's most popular saints. Saint Anthony of Padua, patron saint of lost and stolen articles, was a powerful Franciscan preacher and teacher. He's typically portrayed holding the child Jesus—or a lily, or a book, or all three—in his arms. Many people give alms (traditionally called Saint Anthony Bread) in thanksgiving to God for blessings received through the prayers of Saint Anthony.

Saint Anthony of Padua's life is what every Christian's life is meant to be: a steady courage to face the ups and downs of life, the call to love and forgive, to be concerned for the needs of others, to deal with crises great and small, and to have our feet solidly on the ground of total trusting love and dependence on God.

Saint Anthony is beloved throughout the world and is responsive to all people. As many of the readers know I never spell the word "G-d" with three letters out of respect. For the sake of the actual prayer and for respect I will leave the prayer written as it is:

O blessed Saint Anthony,
the grace of God has made you a powerful advocate
in all our needs and the patron
for the restoring of things lost or stolen.
I turn to you today with childlike love and deep confidence.
You have helped countless children of God
to find the things they have lost,
material things, and, more importantly,
the things of the spirit: faith, hope, and love.
I come to you with confidence;
help me in my present need.
I recommend what I have lost to your care,
in the hope that God will restore it to me,
if it is His holy Will.
Amen.

Lost Earring-Sedona (1995)

In 1995 while working for the US government, I took a trip to Port Hueneme, a small beach city in Ventura, California surrounded by the city of Oxnard and the Santa Barbara Channel.

After being in California for a few weeks and finishing my work, I contacted my friend who lived in Tempe, Arizona and flew out to visit him. We took a few day trips, one to Flagstaff, Arizona and another to visit Sedona, an Arizona desert town surrounded by red rock canyons. While in Sedona I bought Barbara a beautiful pair of turquoise earrings and a matching bracelet. I decided that I wouldn't tell her about it and instead surprise her with them when I got home.

A day or two after I gave her the present, she told me that she lost one of the earrings. Obviously, I didn't have insurance on the earrings so we simply laughed about it.

I didn't know anything about Saint Anthony at the time, but if I had, I would have recited the prayer to try and find the lost earring.

To this day anytime Barbara buys earrings I always jokingly tell her, "Remember Sedona."

Max Bracelet (2006)

Sometime after our son Max passed away on February 18, 2004 at the age of twenty, Barbara decided to make a bracelet with Max's name on it. The clasps were magnetic so she could put it on and off whenever she decided to do so.

Barbara wore the bracelet with pride and as a reminder that even though Max wasn't physically present, he was always in her heart and mind. Barbara is very artsy and has painted and designed lots of jewelry and beaded items with her granddaughter Maya and sometimes by herself. Around 2006 Barbara went shopping in Stop and Shop in the Parkade in Cranston, Rhode Island. I had just got home from work and had not yet changed out of my business suit. She came home when she was done shopping and began to put away the groceries. A few minutes went by and she got a panicked look on her face. I asked her what was troubling her and she said that she couldn't find the bracelet but she was certain that she had it on in Stop and Shop. When she suggested that I call the store my first thought was if someone found it, they probably would keep it. She told me approximately where she parked her car so I could have a starting point for my search.

I told her that even though we are of the Jewish faith we should say the prayer to Saint Anthony to help us locate the bracelet. I silently said the prayer and off I went to Stop and Shop. I arrived at the store and began looking underneath all the cars in the area that Barbara suggested. Within a few minutes I heard someone demand that I get out from underneath the car and I turned around and saw a policeman with his hand on his gun holster. He thought I was breaking into cars but I explained that I was looking for my wife's bracelet. He said "Really?" and asked for my license and registration which I provided to him. I asked if he thought I'd be breaking into cars wearing my suit, and he then said he would help me look.

Just by chance within a minute or so a store employee was pushing some shopping carts in the parking lot and when he saw me, he casually asked if I was looking for a bracelet with the name "Max" on it. I said I was and he came up and hugged me and told me he knew that I would come back to retrieve it. When I asked if I could give him a tip, he said no thank you. I insisted but again he said no. He told me his name was John and he worked two or three days a week at the store.

After I thanked him, I walked into the store and asked for the manager. I told the manager what happened and he said that John was a part-time employee who worked there. I told the manager I wanted to give John a thank-you and a gift and the manager said that John had special needs so he would give the gift to John's parents who usually dropped him off and picked him up. I went home and got my checkbook, wrote a check to John, and gave it to the store manager to give to his parents. John didn't cash the check for over a year. Every time I went to the store and I saw him I told him about the check and he said he didn't want a tip and he wanted to return my check. Finally, he told me if I gave him cash that would be acceptable.

I got cash and I gave it to his parents the next time I came to the store when he was being picked up for his ride home. This small example of kindness has stayed with me for many years and even though I haven't seen John, I still think of his kindness years later.

Lost Wallets–Price Rite (2020) / Walgreens (2022)

These two lost wallet incidents were both solved by me reciting the Saint Anthony prayer. I know that it may sound like I am making this up but I am not.

Lost Wallet–Price Rite (2020)

Before Covid was upon us I was volunteering three to four days a week at various local organizations making breakfast, delivering meals on wheels, and numerous other things. On one of these occasions, I went to the local food bank with a friend of mine to pick up some items that were being donated to a smaller organization to distribute to those in need. On this particular day there weren't enough items to be given out so we decided to go to the Price Rite market on Valley Street in Providence to get the rest. We took two empty carriages and walked all around the store getting what we needed. My friend took out his credit card to pay and we went outside, loaded up his truck, and drove away.

A few minutes went by and I casually asked him if he had the receipt to hand into the organization for reimbursement. He said that he wouldn't seek reimbursement since this was his way of giving back his time and money to help out. He suddenly asked me if his wallet was in the glove box. I checked and it wasn't. He had a sort of panicked look on his face. I calmly told him not to worry and that we should simply drive back to the market. We proceeded back and he kept saying that his entire life was in his wallet.

As we drove back, I told him that I would say a small prayer to find the wallet. He laughed at me and said that I should do what I wanted but the wallet was lost. We got to the store and I asked for a manager. She came over and my friend explained what had happened. The manager took down my friend's name and phone number and he said that it was time to go. As we turned to leave the store, out of nowhere a man came up to the manager and said that he just found a wallet on the floor a few aisles back. Of course, it was my friend's wallet. He handed it over and my friend gave him a sort of finder's fee, and we proceeded out the door. I guess either the prayer worked again or we were at the right place in the right time.

Lost Wallet–Walgreens (2022)

In the spring of 2022, I was visiting my local Walgreens at 1010 Park Avenue in Cranston, Rhode Island to pick up a prescription for myself. I said hi to the usual cast of characters I would always see, including the pharmacist, the pharmacy technicians, and the young lady who runs the photo and beauty counters.

After taking care of my business, I went by the beauty counter and casually said hi to the sales clerk. She seemed a little despondent and when I asked her why, she told me she lost her wallet which held her license, credit card, and all the money from the check that she cashed the day before. She shed a tear or two and I told her not to panic and that she should say Saint Anthony's prayer. She asked me what that was and I explained to her that even though I'm Jewish it's a prayer to find lost items. I told her that I do say it occasionally and I've always been lucky finding things. She told me she didn't really believe in it but she said if I wanted to say the prayer for her it would be fine. I asked her where the wallet was last seen and what it looked like and then I proceeded to say the prayer out loud. I usually would simply say "please help to find the lost items." Some people would rather say the extended prayer but that's their choice. I had a very good feeling that the wallet would be found in the next day and when I would see her again, she would let me know. I told her to attempt to retrace her steps from the last few days to try and find the wallet and she said that she would buy me a Diet Coke to thank me. I said that it wasn't necessary but that would be her decision.

I left the store and felt that the wallet would be found later that day. Getting in my car I decided to drive up and down her street as she'd told me she lived near the store but I had no luck. The next afternoon I went into the store in the afternoon and when she saw me, she put her arms around me and gave me a big hug. She told me that on the way home the night before she went across the street to Burger King to get something to eat after a long day at work. She said she had done this many times. She proceeded to go into the bathroom and wash her hands before walking home. For some strange reason, as she was at the sink, she saw a large amount of paper towels on the counter. She began to pick them up because it looked messy and unbelievably, at the bottom of the pile, was her wallet. She remembered that when she had used the bathroom, she put her wallet down on the counter for a minute or so and then walked out, forgetting it. Just by chance the paper towels covered it up and no one took the cash and credit card. Had she not gone into BK to retrace her steps the wallet and cash would most likely not have been found, at least not by her. As for my reward, I graciously accepted the Diet Coke along with a pack of one of my favorite snacks, marshmallow peeps. The wallet was found and I enjoyed my snacks. The mission was complete once again.

MEDICAL AND HEALTH ISSUES

Seven New Teeth (2023)

As many of the readers may already know I published a book entitled *A Royal Crowning Achievement*. This book was a detailed account of me getting fourteen dental crowns during the time frame of June 29, 2020 through October 31, 2022 due to various dental issues that I had dealt with over the years. The main issue was called "bruxism"; in laymen's terms, grinding of the teeth. Shortly afterwards I left our dentist as he retired. The new dental group located near my home in Cranston, Rhode Island reviewed my medical and dental history and determined that seven additional crowns were needed to complete my treatment plan. Rather than bore you with all the details since I don't want to bite off more than I can chew rehashing it all, suffice it to say that I had teeth numbers 20 and 22 crowned during March 2023, numbers 4, 5, and 6 during April 2023, and numbers 13 and 15 in May 2023. To accomplish all of the above I had many more appointments, x-rays, impressions, and of course Novocain shots. In hindsight I am glad that I did what needed to be done. My advice is to brush and floss after every meal and take care of your teeth before they take a bite out of your time and your wallet. I always took care of my own teeth but age and stress can affect all that you chew on, so to speak.

KEVIN DWARES

More Gum Issues–Take a Bite out of That (2024)

While at the dentist located at Chapel View Boulevard across from the Garden City shopping center in Cranston, Rhode Island on Friday, May 10, 2024, I had my semiannual dental teeth cleaning. All went well for the first ten minutes or so. Suddenly the dentist remarked that my top gums were bleeding profusely, similar to the geyser of oil first discovered by Jed Clampett on *The Beverly Hillbillies* television show on the air in the mid to late 1960s. Obviously when I was told that I would need to see a periodontist to evaluate my gums the words "tooth scaling" and "root planing" were bantered around. I was told that tooth scaling removes tartar from the surface of your teeth that you see when you smile. It doesn't mean a scale to weigh yourself when you think you've gained some pounds and it doesn't mean the scales on a fish. Fish scales are part of the fish's integumentary system, and are produced from the mesoderm layer of the dermis, which distinguishes them from reptile scales. And it doesn't mean the scales on a sheet of music, which are a series of notes ordered by pitch. The notes in a scale belong together and are often used as a basis for melodies and chords in music. Most popular music is based on the notes of one major scale or minor scale, but some pieces of music use different scales along the way.

Then when she once again mentioned the words "root planing" she explained it was the removal of tartar from the roots of your teeth below your gumline.

Planing in dentistry doesn't mean when you fly on a jumbo jet, or planing a piece of wood, which is a fundamental technique in woodworking. Wood planing involves removing thin layers of wood from the surface of a workpiece to create a smooth, even finish. This process is achieved using a specialized tool called a hand plane or a power planer.

I guess now you can tell that scaling and planing can mean many things, but in the dental world, at least in my mind, they mean three things: pain, money to pay the dental professionals, and more pain. As of this story I haven't yet made an appointment for my root planing. I need to go back to the dentist for an additional teeth cleaning in the next few months and a decision will be made then. I hope that the necessary appointments don't take too much of a bite from my credit card. Woof Woof.

MEETING FAMOUS PEOPLE

Richard Nixon (1960)

Do you remember which president left office in disgrace uttering the words "I am not a crook"? These famous words were uttered by none other than "Tricky Dicky" himself, President Richard Nixon. Well, on August 1, 1960, when I was almost five years old, I met the future thirty-seventh president of the United States of America, Richard Milhouse Nixon.

My dad and mom took all five children to visit Richard Nixon at the old Hillsgrove State Airport, now called the Rhode Island T.F. Green International Airport, in Warwick, Rhode Island. He first landed in Warwick prior to his visit to Newport where he spoke at the graduation exercises of the Naval Officer Candidate School. He visited Newport again in March 1971.

A few years later on August 8, 1974, U.S. President Richard Nixon delivered a nationally televised speech to the American public from

the Oval Office announcing his intention to resign the presidency the following day due to the Watergate scandal.

At the age of five I was too young to understand all of this political stuff going on, but I have learned over the years it's not just Democrats, Republicans, or Independents. There are three sides to every story: his, hers, and the truth. Ain't that the truth!

Meeting Lorne Greene (1965)

Lorne Greene was born Lyon Himan "Chaim" Green on February 12, 1915 in Canada. He was on the popular television show *Bonanza* on NBC.

I met him at the opening of an automobile dealership on Taunton Avenue in East Providence, Rhode Island in 1965 while he was visiting a friend from California. The friend's brother lived in Rhode Island and was the one opening the dealership. My dad owned a Chrysler automobile dealership called Philip Dwares Chrysler in Pawtucket, Rhode Island so we were invited to the opening.

I remember to this day that Lorne had a thick head of hair and bushy sideburns. He also wore his trademark vest. He was very pleasant and friendly and signed autographs and graciously took photos with whomever asked him. For many years since our meeting anytime I would head into East Providence I would always remember the time I met Pa, also known as Ben Cartwright from the *Bonanza* television series of the 1960s and 1970s.

Muhammad Ali, (1978)

In January 1978 my late friend Geo was attending law school in Florida and invited me down for a visit. Geo came from a very wealthy family in Cranston, Rhode Island and his family owned and developed a lot of real estate in southern Florida. During my visit we went to Disney World (free tickets) and many other attractions. One afternoon my friend asked me if I wanted to take a ride to Miami to visit a friend of his father's. We enjoyed the ride and ended up in a fairly rundown area at the 5th Street Gym located in Miami Beach. The gym was operated from 1950 to 1993, when it closed. One of the most famous boxers in the world trained there and he was no other than Muhammad Ali. Geo didn't mention it to me but his dad had a lot of financial dealings with the trainers and business partners of Ali.

As we approached the gym, Geo got out to chat with some tall, scary looking guys who all shook his hand and high-fived him. When he motioned for me to get out of his sports car, I initially was afraid not just for me, but that the car wouldn't be there when we returned. A few of his friends hugged me and said something like "If we were to hurt you, it would have been done already." Yes, that made feel more comfortable.

We went inside and walked up the creaky stairs and as soon as we reached the top steps, there he was in the flesh: the man, the myth, the legend who could in the ring float like a butterfly, sting like a bee, the hands can't hit what they can't see. Ali hugged Geo and then came up to me and shook my hand and said I had a nice afro for a white brother. Ali was very cordial and cracked a lot of jokes and allowed us to take a few pictures of him. Unfortunately, the picture of Ali and me is long gone, but you can obviously see the resemblance between him and the good-looking guy I was way back then. We hung around for a while and then headed into Miami for some touring and cruising around. I never forgot the day that I met the man who became famous for his lightning speed in the ring and also for a being a world statesman as he got older. RIP Ali. And Geo.

President Jimmy Carter and Dinner at Mainelli's (1985)

Hurricane Gloria was a powerful Cape Verde hurricane that formed on September 15, 1985 and tracked across the Atlantic through September 28, 1985. It caused a lot of damage, powerful winds, and power losses. Barbara and I were living with our son Max, who was almost two years old at the time, at 154 Irving Ave in Providence's East Side neighborhood near Blackstone Boulevard. We had moved into our apartment in June 1980. We had a great third-floor apartment with a screened in porch. We walked everywhere and truly enjoyed our life.

The news and weather station WJAR Channel 10 Providence kept reporting that a very powerful hurricane would most likely strike the East Coast. Everyone was advised to bring everything in from outside and tape their windows from the inside in case they cracked. This would prevent glass from shattering and getting inside where it could hurt people, animals, or property.

We had already put in an offer to purchase our first house in Cranston and we were set to close on it in mid-October 1985. We went to sleep the night of the storm and kept Max next to us to keep him safe.

The winds were howling all night long as we fell asleep. We woke up in the morning and realized there was no power anywhere. No one knows when or how, but the porch screen got sucked completely out the window and it was down the street somewhere. A very large tree crashed into the house next door to our apartment building and caused a lot of damage.

Luckily, we were prepared somewhat as we had purchased many bottles of water and shelf stable items of food in the days before the storm so we had plenty to eat and drink for at least a few days.

On day three after the storm had passed, I called my insurance company and told them that we still had no power and that I would initiate a claim for everything that was lost. If I recall, a month or so after the storm ended, they sent me a check, I believe for around $200. They didn't ask me for any receipts but assumed that since we had no power for a week that everything in the fridge and freezer and the items in all our cupboards must have spoiled.

On day three or four after the storm left Rhode Island, we were hungry so we decided to call to see if any restaurants were open. The one we found was our favorite called Mainelli's, located on Chalkstone Avenue in Providence. We had been there many times before and it was open, which was the most important thing on my mind.

We asked if we could come in for dinner and they said okay, but to be there no later than 6:00 p.m. since they planned to close early.

We drove to the restaurant and the first thing we noticed was the five to six very big men in the parking lot with hearing aids on, or so we thought.

We wondered why the association for the hard of hearing would be having a meeting that night but we still went in the restaurant and minded our own business.

We said hi to the owners and our favorite waiter and he sat us down in the back room and said he would return to take our order. A few minutes went by and some friends of ours from Barrington also came to the restaurant and were put at the table right behind us.

A few minutes later I see four of these hulks come in the restaurant. Two of them went to the bathroom and two went to the kitchen which we thought was very odd.

It's not my business to be nosy so I didn't say anything, but I wondered what was going on. A few minutes later, believe it or not, in walked former president Jimmy Carter with his daughter Amy and another friend.

They said hi when they sat down—directly across from us!—and ordered dinner. Soon thereafter while we started eating former president Carter got up from the table. He came over and patted Max on his head and saw that he was twirling a spoon. He asked if it was okay to feed a little food to Max and, once I said yes, he picked up the fork on the table and helped to feed Max.

I asked the former president what he was doing in Rhode Island and he said he was visiting his daughter Amy at Brown University where she was a student. He then said they decided to come to this restaurant for dinner since it had a good reputation.

He asked me what I did. When I said I was a federal employee he was very happy and said it was people like me who did a good job as civilians, that we helped the military when they were defending us here and abroad.

Time went on as we were eating and I did think about asking for his autograph but then I decided it wasn't appropriate.

When we were ready to leave and stood up, four of the hulks (Secret Service agents) got up immediately and stood in front of the president. He told them to sit down and not to worry.

I extended my hand to shake his and we left the restaurant. We thought that was the end of the story, but it wasn't.

As many of you know there's never an end to the storytelling when it comes to me. I try to keep it short and not repeat myself, but sometimes I go on and on, if you get my meaning. The following week my friend who was at dinner with us went to the airport to pick up or drop someone off; I can't recall which this many years later. When he was about ready to leave Amy Carter came up to him and said that she remembered him from the restaurant the week before. He asked where her security detail was and he was told that she ditched them in Washington and got on the plane to come back to Providence on her own. However, she had no money on her so she asked my friend to give her a ride back to her dormitory at Brown University.

During their conversation on the way there, she said she hated being in Washington, D.C. and she liked Providence, Rhode Island since it was quaint and quiet and she could be herself.

He dropped her off and that was the last he ever heard from her.

I guess the way the story ends is that Amy went back to Brown but in 1987 she was asked to leave due to failing grades and ended up going to another college to graduate. She later earned a degree from the Memphis College of Art and later on a master's degree from Tulane in 1996. The real story of that night was how the hurricane brought me and my friends together at a restaurant to have dinner with a president and to bring the president's daughter home to her dorm room safely. All ended well and that's the rest of the story.

Meeting President George H.W. Bush 41st U.S. President (1989)

While employed at the United States Naval War College from the mid-1990s until my retirement I had the opportunity to visit and meet with numerous military members who spent many years as prisoners of war in Vietnam. I also was able to meet many well-known dignitaries including President H.W. Bush, the forty-first US president.

George Herbert Walker Bush was born on June 12, 1924 and passed away on November 30, 2018. Prior to him being elected he also was a diplomat, and a very successful businessman as well. I won't talk about my personal feelings on his presidency but of the man that I met when he visited my place of employment.

He was at the Naval War College to give a speech regarding global tensions in the Middle East and the Far East and was to meet with family members of military men and women who were killed in action while serving our country. My department was involved in the planning and execution of the presidential visit but not from any security standpoint. A few months prior to his arrival an advance team of members of his staff came to our department with requests and many, many recommendations that needed to be implemented prior to his visit. I can't get into any details but needless to say the advance team and my group worked long and hard to make sure the visit went off without any issues. We were told that the visit would last less than one hour and the budget to make his visit safe and secure was unlimited. In the weeks before his arrival a special staircase was built inside one of the buildings so he could be protected at all times. In the auditorium a special door was erected for a quick exit and the podium around was super protected as well just in case. I was a little nervous. I was vetted by security to be in the general vicinity but rest assured, I had no direct access unless the president decided to approach me to shake my hand.

Two minutes or so before his speech, he was ushered in by many security personnel and to my great surprise came down the stairs close to where I was waiting for my admittance to the auditorium. As he turned, I extended my hand; he shook it with a steady and determined grasp and simply said "Thank you for your service to our country." When I mentioned that I was a civilian he said that my job was just as important as our support was also crucial to the "war fighters." He was very dignified and well-spoken and I went home feeling proud that I was an American. That's my short story and I am sticking to it. G-d Bless America and our troops.

Jack Klugman (Washington D.C.) (1999)

Somewhere around 1999 my wife Barbara and I took a road trip from Cranston to Falls Church, Virginia to visit Barbara's sister.

One of the days of our visit we took the Metro into D.C. and then boarded a tour bus that went around all the Smithsonians and downtown Washington. Passengers could get off and on at numerous stops along the way. While we were walking near the White House, we saw a man walking around by himself who looked very familiar. As he came close to us, I realized he was Jack Klugman, the actor—or a man who looked like the actor—who played Oscar Madison in the television show *The Odd Couple*. In case you don't remember, the show starred Tony Randall as Felix Unger and Jack Klugman as Oscar Madison. It was about two divorced men who live together, and whose contrasting personalities inevitably lead to conflict and laughter. We chatted for a minute or so and he continued on his stroll around the Washington, D.C. area. He died December 24, 2012 at the age of ninety.

Meeting President George W. Bush 43rd U.S. President (2007)

Dubya—the folksy Texan pronunciation of his middle initial W.—was used to distinguish the son from the father as both George Bushes ended up as presidents of the United States. The forty-third president was in my own opinion far different from his dad. George Walker Bush was born on July 6, 1946 and was the president from 2001 to 2009. Prior to his time in office, he also was the forty-sixth governor of Texas from 1995 through 2000.

I met the forty-third president by chance as he was at the US Naval War College as a speaker at one of the yearly graduation ceremonies. I wasn't allowed to attend this ceremony as I did when the forty-first president was here due to the limited number of guests allowed. Sometime before his arrival I was tasked by the director of my agency to bring the certificates that were to be given to the "Gold Star families" up to the admiral's office. The Gold Star family is one that has experienced a loss of a loved one—an immediate family member—who died as the result of active-duty military service. Those who die in service to their country leave behind parents, siblings, spouses, children, and extended families. These are recognized as Gold Star families. The title is meant to honor the service member's ultimate sacrifice while acknowledging their family's loss, grief, and continued healing. **Since 9/11, more than sixteen thousand troops have died in non-combat circumstances and more than seven thousand died in the Iraq and Afghanistan wars alone.** There are also thousands of living Gold Star family members who lost loved ones in both world wars, the Korean War, the Vietnam War, and other conflicts.

Walking into the office I saw the admiral's aide and I handed him the certificates; then glanced to the right, and saw the president having a drink of water. He motioned to me and came over and shook my hand and said hello. I responded and then I was asked by the admiral's aide to leave the room since the meeting between the president and the Gold Star families was set to begin. I left and went back down to my office and told everyone about my good fortune of meeting a president.

May those who made the ultimate sacrifice rest in peace.

G-d Bless America and May G-d Bless our troops.

Meeting Jay Leno (2018)

In the summer of 2018 me and my wife Barbara plus my son Jake, his wife Maria, and our granddaughter Maya took a one-week vacation to New Hampshire. While enjoying ourselves we took in the beautiful scenery, ate in many restaurants, and took many day trips. We took the world famous Cog Railway to the summit of Mount Washington, took some hikes, rode ski lifts up to the top of mountains, and on one occasion we took a ride to visit the Mount Washington Hotel.

This hotel in Bretton Woods, New Hampshire is part of a land grant made in 1772 by Royal Governor John Wentworth. The area was named after Bretton Hall, Wentworth's ancestral home in Yorkshire, England. The hotel was built by New Hampshire native Joseph Stickney, who made his fortune in coal mining and the Pennsylvania Railroad. Stickney spared no expense in building the imposing hotel. To this day, the Bretton Woods Hotel has its own private telephone system and post office. The hotel has been host to Thomas Edison, three US presidents, and countless other celebrities as well, such as Joe Kennedy, Princess Margaret, John D. Rockefeller, and of course my favorite, Jay Leno.

During our visit to the hotel, we first parked our car then walked up the long walkway to the front porch of the hotel. As soon as we'd climbed the stairs, I noticed a familiar face walking right by me holding a drink in his hand. When a family in front of us said "Jay Leno"

that confirmed it. Instead of him being dressed in his trademark suit he wore simple jeans and a jean top. He was very gracious to everyone and I offered to take his picture with the family who saw him before we did. As soon as I was done taking the photos I asked the family to take a picture of Barbara and me with the one and only Jay Leno. I asked him why he was visiting New Hampshire and he said that he was participating in a road race up to the top of Mount Washington on the auto road with his steam-powered car. After our short chat we proceeded to take a short tour inside the hotel and then went out on the back patio with its expansive lawns and had a few drinks and snacks. The photo with "Jay" and the relaxing afternoon made the trip to New Hampshire worth it.

Meeting Jesus or a Lookalike (2019)

Disclaimer: Before I begin my short story about meeting someone who looked and acted like Jesus himself, I want to tell the reader that I am not trying to be funny or disrespectful. I am simply telling you what I saw back in the summer of 2019 and the events that transpired that day.

In the summer of 2019, my wife and I were invited to a craft fair in Mattapoisett, Massachusetts. There were many booths set up as people were selling jewelry and many other fine arts and crafts. While walking around I decided to get a drink of soda and some French fries and I noticed a lot of people surrounding a person walking down one of the pathways.

I decided to see what was going on and believe it or not I saw a man who looked exactly like Jesus Christ himself. He was walking in a long white robe and carrying a walking stick; I also noticed that he had a crown of thorns on his head and he was bleeding. While I did actually think that he was simply dressed up like Jesus I went up to him and introduced myself. I told him that I was of the Jewish faith and he softly told me that he was born Jewish and that he was indeed who I thought he was. I asked if he would mind if I could take a picture of him and myself and he obliged. We chatted for a few minutes and he told me with a straight face that he indeed was "HIM."

I asked him if I could be honest and he said of course. I then told him that Judaism does not accept Jesus as a divine being, an intermediary between humans and God, a messiah, or holy. Belief in the trinity is also held to be incompatible with Judaism, as are a number of other tenets of Christianity. He went on to tell me that most Christians believe that Jesus was both human and the Son of God. I told him that when I got home, I would do some research on G-d and Jesus. He hugged me and softly kissed me on the top of my head and said "G-d Bless you." He walked away to talk to other people at the craft fair.

While I stood watching him slowly walk down a path a policeman came up to me and asked what I chatted about with Jesus. I told him we chatted about life in general. When I asked the officer who he thought the man who looked like Jesus was, he thought it was a local man with mental health issues. The officer simply smiled and said that he would leave it up to me to decide who I actually met that day. To this very day, anytime I see anyone who looks homeless or potentially has mental health issues, I always think back to the day I met a man who looked like Jesus, and perhaps he may very well have been. Who am I to say?

I don't claim to have any answers pertaining to Jesus, G-d, the holy trinity or anything else. I can only be the best person that I can be and live a good life to the fullest. Someday perhaps when I leave the earthly confines of my life I will learn and hear the truth about the very existence of life itself. Or perhaps a famous movie quote may say it all: "You can't handle the truth."

MEETING THE WOMAN WHO WOULD CHANGE MY WORLD

Meeting Barbara Due to the Connections with Sheryl (Marks) Ishai

During the summers from 1955 when I was born until the death of my dad in 1968 my family would rent a large beach house in Narragansett, Rhode Island. It was located right off Ocean Road on 10 Rodman Street. It was a great place to have a large family, and have cookouts and parties, and to meet new and exciting people, some of whom I still stay in touch with. It also played a crucial role in me meeting my future wife many years later. On the property was a large house and a smaller home that other families would rent. We became very close to one of the families and the daughter of that family became Barbara's college roommate and would accompany Barbara to Israel many years later to volunteer in a development town teaching immigrant children. That connection is how I met my future wife. Without that simple yet very powerful connection, life may have turned out very differently.

To give you a somewhat brief but slightly complicated history, in 1972, Barbara enrolled at the University of Rhode Island and in 1976 earned a bachelor of arts (BA) elementary education degree. She met Sheryl Marks, formerly of Pawtucket, Rhode Island, who would later become Sheryl Ishai who now lives in the coastal city of Ashkelon, Israel located on the Mediterranean coast. Barbara and Sheryl became roommates and lived in Gorman Hall. After Barbara's graduation she lived in Bonnet Shores in Narragansett, Rhode Island with some friends from May 1976 to February 1977 and worked as a waitress and at other part-time jobs. In February 1977 she went to Israel with Sheryl and they lived and worked in Dimona, Israel teaching children. Dimona is a town of the Negev region in southern Israel. Allegedly, Israel developed a nuclear weapon at the Negev Nuclear Research Center which even today they will neither deny or confirm. Barbara and Sheryl remained in Israel until February 1978 when Barbara moved back into her family's home in Cranston, Rhode Island. She then worked part time until September 1978 teaching Hebrew school and then moved back to Narragansett.

Barbara and I met on March 11, 1979 and she moved back home once again in June 1979. At this time, she substituted statewide in elementary schools. In September 1979 she began working at the Jewish Community Center (JCC) in Providence where she taught preschool. We married on June 29, 1980 and Barbara continued to teach preschool and Hebrew school until June 1986.

First Date at Bowling Alley Breakfast (March 11, 1979)

To digress slightly I want to tell you how we met and the occasion that would eventually lead up to it. Sometime in early February 1979 I woke up with a bad sore throat and rather than call my doctor I decided to take a ride to the pharmacy to get some cough medicine. I usually went to a store nearby but for some unknown reason I drove to the other side of Cranston and ended up going to a now defunct pharmacy called Adams Drugs. I had never been there before but decided to go in. I went to the back of the store and lo and behold, I saw the pharmacist who worked there. He was the father of the young girl that I had met many years ago in Narragansett who would become Barbara's college roommate and travel with her to Israel. She also, due to fate, became the person who eventually brought me and Barbara together as husband and wife and as lifelong friends.

While I was in the store the pharmacist asked me how life was going. I told him that I had finished my education and was considering moving to Israel to make a life for myself. He explained that his daughter Sheryl Marks (now known as Sheryl Ishai) and her friend Barbara Gold (now Barbara Gold Dwares) had both returned from Israel after spending the last year teaching children. He gave me Barbara's parents' phone number and I promised that I would call her in the next few days. I did call her home and left a message and when I didn't hear back, I figured I was done trying. Boy, that would have been a big mistake for me.

A day or so later I got a message back from her asking me if I was a marshmallow and didn't have the courage to call her back. She said that her parents left a message on the kitchen refrigerator that said a Kevin Dwares called and that he would call back the following week. I decided to call her and she said that she was living in her parents' home in Cranston and I could pick her up the next day. Just to be safe in case it didn't work out, I brought my fishing rod with me to go fishing and kept it between us as sort of a dividing line.

I arrived at her house and this cute, adorable young lady opened the door and I shyly said hi it's me Kevin, to which she replied something like, who else would it be? We got into my fairly new Honda Accord and began the drive.

No sooner had we got on Route 95 heading south than she asked me if I minded if she lit up a cigarette. I thought about it and reluctantly said it was fine even though back then and even now I hate the smell of tobacco. She lit up but I decided to open all of the car windows to let out the smoke. After a few minutes of casual conversation, she threw the lit cigarette out the window and it blew back into the back window and burned a nice sized hole in my back seat. I could smell the seat burning so I pulled over to investigate. She said that she was sorry and I thought for a second or so that I could leave her and drive off but decided that was not the proper or nice thing to do. Instead, we went to a local bowling alley in Wakefield, Rhode Island which also included a diner. Today it is called Old Mountain Lanes.

We ordered a late breakfast and chatted and after a while we really began to click and hit it off. I thoroughly enjoyed her company and decided to ask her out on a real date in the next few days. I brought her back to her house at the beach in Narragansett that she rented with a few of her girlfriends.

We began to date and a little more than a year later we were married; at the time of this story we have been married over forty-four years. As for Barbara and Sheryl, they have remained good friends even though she and her husband Shmuel now live in Israel. Barbara has visited Sheryl many times in Israel, and Sheryl and her husband have stayed with us in Rhode Island every time they have come to the United States for a visit.

Second Date at Bowling Alley Breakfast (June 30, 2024)

It's hard to believe that over forty-four years later Barbara and I celebrated our second date at the same bowling alley that we met at in 1979. This time however we were joined by close to forty-five of our closest friends. I had given considerable thought to having a surprise

party for Barbara but she doesn't enjoy those type of surprises. Instead, I contacted the alley for all of the pertinent details and sat down one night with her in early March 2024 and sprung the idea on her. She immediately told me that she loved it and was glad that I thought of a great, unique idea for our anniversary.

Due to Covid from 2020 through and including 2024 we weren't able to have a celebration. I even sprung the idea of a get-together in the Newport Creamery parking lot in Garden City located in Cranston, Rhode Island, but that was rained out as well. The Old Mountain Lanes idea seemed to be the best since the place obviously has significance to us and is an ideal location. We made plans to have a simple buffet breakfast and to invite some of our closest friends and relatives, which numbered seventy-five. Around forty-five people actually showed up to join in our celebration. Here's one down memory lane, pun intended.

MONEY, MONEY, MONEY

Insurance Scam $10,000 Engagement Ring at Golf Driving Range (1975)

Many years ago, an old family friend of mine that I will call Steve invited me and a few other friends to a golf range in Seekonk, Massachusetts. Steve was around five or so years older than me. He let us in on a surprise. When we got to the range, he told us that he was going to ask his longtime girlfriend to marry him and we were all going to be in his wedding party. He proceeded to take a little box out of his pocket and inside was the beautiful diamond ring he was going to give to her. He put the ring on his finger and we responded that it was beautiful. He then told us he purchased it for $10,000. We spent the next few hours banging the balls out onto the open range. On the way home Steve told us that he couldn't find the ring and that it must have fallen off while he was putting some balls. We turned around to try and find the ring but by the time we got back it was getting dark. He told the golf manager who called the police to let them know in case the ring was located. The next day he called and told us the police would be contacting us, as well as his insurance company. Sure enough, in the next few days we all were called by the police and the insurance company to give our sides of the story.

Well, a month or so later my friend told me that he received a check from his insurance company for $10,000 to compensate him for the lost ring. A few months went by and my friend was married and none of his friends, including me, were invited to his wedding. Steve and his new wife moved out of town and I thought I would never see him again.

Many years passed by and my wife and I were visiting Costco in Sharon, Massachusetts. Out of nowhere a man came up to me who I didn't recognize. He said that he was Steve from many years ago and by this stage he was balding, had a potbelly, and was hunched over. We got reacquainted and I asked him about the ring incident. He had a smile on his face and said, thank you very much for what I did, and when I asked him what he meant, he said that I was a witness to the ring that was lost. He then said thank G-d the statute of limitations was over because he never lost the ring, he simply told his insurance company he lost it so he could put in an insurance claim. Once it was settled, he had a down payment for the house he was purchasing. He then said that he invited me and the other friends out that night years back to act as witnesses to the insurance fraud that he'd planned on committing. He used us as witnesses for a crime.

I told him that wasn't the right thing to do and he said it was nice seeing me again and I never saw him again. The moral of this story: If you ever get invited to a golf range and someone asks you to look at the ring that he bought for his wife, ignore him and turn the other way.

Boat Insurance Fraud (1976)

What I was around twenty years old, an older relative of mine named Lou was visiting Rhode Island for the summer with his family after living in Los Angeles, California for the last thirty years or so. He was in the art business and from what my mom told me he was very wealthy but slightly arrogant as well. He had his forty-foot cabin cruiser shipped from California and kept it docked at a slip at a yacht club near Narragansett, Rhode Island and invited me to stay on his boat overnight.

We spent the day cruising around and dropped anchor in Galilee which is a small fishing village with a lot of boats and great seafood restaurants. It was then and still is very popular. From there, you can also take the ferry to Block Island, a short one-hour ride and twelve miles away.

Cousin Lou stocked the boat with all types of food, snacks, and drinks, and we went cruising around the area before we settled in for the cookout that night about a ten-minute ride from the dock. We were going to anchor close to where the Block Island ferry came in and out of Galilee.

Lou dropped the anchor and he lit the small grill to cook hotdogs and hamburgers. Around 9:30 p.m. I was tired so I went downstairs into the cabin and began to drift off to sleep. Within ten minutes or so I heard Lou screaming for me to put on my life jacket as the boat was filling up with water.

I climbed up the stairs as quickly as I could and tried hard not to panic. Within a minute at the most a boat came out of nowhere and a man on board yelled for us to jump on which we immediately did. We were lifted on to his boat and within five or so minutes our boat disappeared into the deep blue sea. Boy, were we lucky that a boat was nearby!

That night gave me an exciting (and terrifying) story to tell...but let me tell you the *rest* of it. I didn't realize at the time but the man on the boat was Lou's friend and they had planned to sink the boat that night to collect on the insurance. Lou's friend called the Coast Guard from his onboard radio and we waited for them to arrive. I told them what happened and of course I didn't realize what was going on at the time since I was young and dumb. Lou used me to pull off what we now call an insurance scam. I didn't find out the truth until years later.

When I was about twenty-five years old Lou was once again visiting family in Rhode Island and I bumped into him at a family gathering and he asked how I was doing. He began to tell the story from a few years back. He told me the truth; that he sank the boat with an accomplice for an insurance payout and that it was very common in the boating industry. He explained that boats depreciate dramatically after purchase and if you want to sell an old boat you may get 50 or 75 percent less than you bought it for.

He told me that as I was beginning to fall asleep, he signaled his friend in his boat nearby, and he himself pulled the plug in the bottom of his own boat, letting it slowly fill with water. I asked him how much he received from his insurance company. With a cocky smile he replied more than $50K.

I told him that he was a piece of shit and asked him how he could take such a risk with someone's (my!) life. He simply said I was being too dramatic. I recently heard that he passed away.

Paying Off Mortgage (1990)

Barbara and I bought our first house in October 1985 after spending five years in our apartment on Irving Avenue on the East Side. Way back then houses cost anywhere between $40,000 and $60,000. Our budget at the time I believe was that we could afford a house that cost $60,000 or less based upon just my salary, and that we could save Barbara's salary to pay bills and pay our mortgage off as soon as we could. We settled on a small house in Cranston, Rhode Island that was involved in bankruptcy. It happened that my uncle was a bankruptcy judge at the time and also would act as our real estate attorney. I asked him for some pertinent information about the house but he declined to provide it to me because it would be a conflict of interest for him to get involved. We met the realtor at the house in Cranston, looked at the house, and we immediately decided to buy the property since there was a cat flap on the porch so we could let our cat in and outside as often as it wanted.

I did a market survey of housing values and we decided to offer $56,900, which was immediately accepted. At the closing there was a disagreement as to who would pay for the oil remaining in the oil tank but other than that the mortgage was initiated and the closing went off without a hitch. Immediately after we left the bank we went to the house with a small moving truck and we noticed that the garage door opener, which was electronic, and the antenna on the roof were missing. I contacted my uncle to explain what happened and he said it would cost more money to get these issues resolved and just to forget about it. We moved into the house that day and thoroughly enjoyed it for close to thirty-two years before we sold it and moved to another home in Garden City, Cranston.

Now for the rest of the story. I was working as a full-time federal employee and Barbara was a school teacher. We decided that we would pay off the mortgage as soon as possible. We took a thirty-year mortgage but we promised ourselves that we would pay that mortgage off in five years or less. Every time we had a pay raise we would put that money towards the principal of our house. Believe me it wasn't easy because we gave up taking vacations and other things, but we were determined to pay that mortgage off in five years or less. Sometime around 1990 a few months shy of our goal we finally paid the mortgage off.

I thought realistically that life was going to be wonderful from there forward. I was told by the mortgage company that I would get some release of mortgage paperwork and it would also be sent to the local city hall. It would take two or three weeks for this to occur. I was dancing on air because I thought we had made the biggest accomplishment ever. We were so excited. One great day the envelope came, I opened it up, and there was a release of mortgage certificate embossed by the mortgage company as well as the city records department. For a few minutes or so I felt like a millionaire since we had no mortgage at a young age and an extra $500 or so a month to spend (the amount of our monthly mortgage payments).

Now for the rest of the story. The next morning, I woke up, and to be quite honest I felt exactly as I had the day before, the difference being we didn't have a mortgage payment. Our life would still continue with the same good times and bad times that everyone else would have. I felt no different that day moving forward without a mortgage. I guess the lesson for me was that money is important to pay bills or pay a mortgage off early. However, it didn't change me at all. I guess having money and having limited debt is beneficial but that's all.

Money, I have learned, can never buy you happiness or health. It's simply a tool to use to one's advantage if you can. Of course, I'd rather have money than not, but it's only a means to an end, nothing more and nothing less. I will leave you with this thought. An extremely wealthy man once told me that having enormous amounts of money may let you buy a bigger house or a more expensive suit, car, or steak dinner. However, a person can only put on their pants one leg at a time. He ended our conversation with the following thoughts: The only thing guaranteed in life is death and taxes. We all came from dust and we end as dust. Live to the Max.

Attempted Boat Sinking–Wealthy Doctor (2000)

Somewhere around 2000 in Rhode Island, a friend of mine who was a well-known radiologist and his wife invited Barbara and I to go out on his cabin cruiser; or as I like to say, live the life of Thurston Howell III from the television show *Gilligan's Island*. My friend told me that he paid $350,000 for this boat which was probably forty to fifty feet long. Inside the boat downstairs was a full-size refrigerator and couch and other amenities. I was jealous at first but quickly got over that when he began to complain how expensive it was to maintain his toy.

In the front of the boat were two bedrooms, each having bunk beds, and the master bedroom, which was huge in size, along with a full-size shower. Up on the top deck was the navigation system and all the radar equipment. As I mentioned I was a little envious, but we were out with our friends to celebrate the Fourth of July in Bristol, Rhode Island.

My friend stocked the boat with all types of alcohol, snacks, steaks, and burgers. Down in the galley was a full kitchen which included a stove and other amenities. He also had a gas grill that he was going to light up once we got to our spot overlooking the location of the Fourth of July Bristol, Rhode Island fireworks.

We had a great time and he even let me sit in the captain's chair and steer the boat. For a little bit, I got to go fast or slow down or go left or right. It was fun.

When we arrived at the spot we could watch fireworks, he dropped the anchor and radioed some of his friends nearby to get close to his boat and tie up, like an outdoor block party. While having my steak and drinking my favorite Diet Coke, my friend casually said to me that maintaining that boat was very expensive. He said that it costs a fortune for gas, maintenance, upkeep, and insurance. He then asked if I was interested in making ten to fifteen thousand in cash. When I asked him why he simply said if I could have someone sink his boat; then he would put a claim to his insurance company for close to half a million dollars. Of course, I laughed and thought he was joking. He said the boat cost $350,000 plus all the extra electronics and everything else in it and he was fully if not overly insured.

I told him I wasn't interested in that, and he said to me that since I worked for the government, he thought I would know some people who would be willing to make some money helping him make his boat disappear. He went on to tell me of an elaborate plan he'd thought up, which would include me coming out on his boat for a weekend for a prearranged fishing trip. While we were out fishing way past Block Island, he would have his friends come and pick us up and at the same time he would scuttle the boat and cause it to sink. In case you're not familiar to scuttle a boat means to sink it deliberately, especially by opening seacocks or making openings in the hull. A seacock is a valve on the hull of a boat or a ship, permitting water to flow into the vessel when needed, such as for cooling an engine. After the boat began to sink he said we would continue to fish for the rest of the weekend about five to ten miles off Block Island. He would make sure that the boat would sink and that there was no evidence of what happened. His friend nearby would call the Coast Guard to say that they rescued some fishermen from a sinking boat. I told my friend that he was nuts and I wanted no involvement.

He told me that he was having problems paying his bills as his medical career was on a downward spiral. I emphatically told him I had no interest in getting involved with something so stupid and illegal.

With a cocky grin on his shit-eating face he told me it was not a problem, but since I was not considered a friend anymore, Barbara and I would never go on his boat again.

A few years went by and I heard that the doctor friend of mine lost his license since he and his wife were fraudulently billing Medicare or Medicaid for unnecessary radiology tests.

Anytime we went over to his house even before this incident, I always had an uneasy feeling, the hair going up on the back of my neck. He used to say stuff about how life was so expensive and he wished that he could get rid of his two Jaguars and other things but I never took it seriously. Had I thought about it further I probably would not have gone on the boat with him but needless to say I never heard from him again and I'm happy about that.

I guess I could end the story by simply saying that the captain of the ship didn't go down with the ship, which was a long-standing maritime tradition. However, in the end he did go down with the ship. Since he billed insurance companies for medical work not done, he lost his license to practice medicine. I also just recently heard that he passed away a few months ago.

Gambling $1,800 Twice and $700 with Max (2002)

Back in early 2002 Barbara and I adopted a greyhound named Savannah at the former Lincoln Greyhound Park, now known as Twin River Casino in Lincoln, Rhode Island.

Savannah was a good dog but could be stubborn at times. The veterinarian we used had her office located across the street from the casino. On one of these visits a friend of mine called and told me he was gambling at the casino. He asked me to come over to gamble but I told him I didn't gamble and I also didn't like the stench of cigarette smoke in the casino. He said he would give me ten dollars to give it a try and if I won the proceeds would be all mine. I told him a few times that I wasn't interested but eventually I reluctantly agreed and went across the street while Barbara kept the appointment with the dog.

The friend took me over to the slot machines and told me to watch for somebody doing some weird finger movements on the screen, as well as rubbing lucky rabbit's feet. I thought that he was joking but he wasn't. I watched the other gamblers and sure enough, within a few minutes I saw a woman moving her fingertips across the machine in an X, kissing a rabbit's foot for luck. I asked her what she was doing and she told me to take two fingers and make an X on her machine when she was done and kiss her rabbit's foot. I thought she was a little loony but I did what she said. She got up to go to another machine and I immediately sat down in front of the slot machine. I put the ten dollars in and pulled the handle and I heard bells and whistles going off; I assumed I won ten or twenty dollars. In a few minutes an employee came over to me and said I won $1,800. I was escorted to the winner's window and after providing my license and social security card they gave me my $1,800 and a tax form so I could declare my income to pay taxes at the end of the year.

Immediately after, I left the casino, walked across the street, and told Barbara, then we left. We called Max, who was visiting friends on the East Side, gave him a hundred-dollar bill, and told him to treat his friends for lunch. Max had been diagnosed with leukemia on March 8, 2001 so when he was feeling good, he would hang out with his friends on the East Side and go to lunch and chat.

A few days later I went back to the casino, again with ten dollars, and I went to the same machine and did the same movements with my fingers on the screen. I put the ten dollars in the machine and pulled the handle and I won $1,800 again. I knew that this was my lucky day so I once again cashed in my winnings and left the casino immediately, then headed home.

On August 11, 2002 I kept the promise that I made to Max to take him skydiving a year after his bone marrow transplant to cure him of leukemia. (See story in table of contents entitled Parachute with Max). That was the day we both were to jump out of a perfectly good airplane. We had a great time. After we both landed, Max asked me if we could go gambling across the street. I said of course, even though he was fragile, frail, and obviously tired.

He knew the story of my two previous wins so I gave him a ten-dollar bill and we proceeded to the same machine I had won at on the two previous times.

I know the reader may think I am full of shit but yes, Max won. Not $1,800 but $700. He was so happy and excited. I went to cash out his winnings in my name so he wouldn't have any tax obligations. I gave him the total amount of $700 to spend any way he chose to. Before we left, we went to the food court at the casino and I treated even though Max told me he would pay the bill. He asked me to take him back again in the future and I said that I would do so.

After that day Max was in and out of the hospital many more times and I never had the opportunity to take him gambling again. To be honest, I was crying when writing this short story. It brought back a very sad chapter in my life as well as others. Barbara and many other family members and friends of ours were very upset with me for taking Max skydiving. While Barbara, Jake, and everyone else had no idea what we were doing I don't regret it for a minute.

It did take some coordinating on my behalf to pull this off. I had a friend in Florida invite Barbara and Jake to visit for a week or so to get them away since I am sure that they didn't and wouldn't approve of my plans.

Needless to say, I did ask the medical staff if it was okay to take Max skydiving and they reluctantly agreed but I had to make sure that we jumped from no higher than ten thousand feet. I asked them why and they gave me some medical data and statistics which said that there was a high chance that Max would be fine but that the final decision was both Max's and mine. When I told Max that we were going to jump out of a perfectly good airplane the look on Max's face was priceless. One thing that Max said to me was "Dad, we had better land safely or Mom will kill us both."

While we were both scared shitless, when we landed, we both let out a loud yahoo and hugged each other and cried. We had done it and I kept the promise to my dying son. Do I ever have any regrets from the day that I took Max skydiving? The answer is simple: NO. Max was ill and lived his life like a true champion. He almost never had a negative attitude during the three long years that he was ill. Even though he battled a terrible fucking disease he kept his belief in G-d and mankind always in a forward and positive approach to life.

I have learned a lot from Max as well as from my younger son Jake. While Max obviously isn't here and only lived a short twenty years, both of them ARE always my true heroes. They both live(d) life to the fullest, almost always staying positive. Both Barbara and I are blessed with having the greatest children, grandchild (Maya), and daughter-in-law (Maria) that anyone could ever want.

I leave you with the expressions that I like to conclude with: Live life to the fullest. Life is the journey not the destination. Live to the Max. *L'chaim.*

SHEKELS—MONETARY UNIT OF ISRAEL/US DOLLARS

2001 Gansett Ave Cranston (Boston Sub)

On a Saturday in 2001 I was taking a walk near my house and I went by Boston Sub, a local sandwich shop located on Gansett Ave in Cranston. (It has since gone out of business.)

As I was humming and softly singing to myself, I looked down and noticed a large women's wallet in the parking lot. I of course immediately picked it up. It was stuffed with hundred-dollar bills. I looked at the name on her license. I decided to go into the sub shop and I asked the manager if he knew the woman. He said no but suddenly a woman got up from her booth and said that she overheard my conversation and that it was her. Obviously, I didn't know if it was her or not, so I asked her for her street address, which I verified by looking at the license.

She was very thankful that I found her wallet because she had just taken out $4,000 from the bank for a family vacation in a few days. She then told me she wanted to give me a $100 tip and buy me lunch which I politely declined. She asked me why I wouldn't take the tip or get a sandwich and I told her that it wouldn't be right and that people should return things and not expect anything in return.

She asked me again and then told me that it's nice that there are people like me in the world and she appreciated it. This wouldn't be the last time that I would find a wallet or money.

2010 Gansett Ave Cranston (Disney Trip)

On one of my daily walks, I went down Packard Street in Cranston and took a right on Gansett Ave. I was walking past a Korean and Japanese restaurant. My wife and I have eaten there many times since. It's a family-operated authentic Japanese and Korean restaurant featuring sushi rolls, noodle dishes, and Korean dishes. Once again, I was humming to myself while walking past the parking lot when I noticed a wallet on the ground. I looked in it and it was stuffed with hundred-dollar bills along with information about Disney World. I saw a driver's license in it and I went inside the restaurant to ask if they knew the person whose name was on it. They did not. I went home and looked in the phone book and called at least ten people whose names matched.

I finally located the correct person and they told me they would meet me at 10:00 p.m. the same night in front of the restaurant.

At ten o'clock sharp I was in front and a couple pulled up and got out. I extended my hand and the husband and wife didn't accept my handshake. They opened the wallet in front of me and counted the cash and said it was a good thing that the $900 was still there. I asked them if they thought I would steal some money and then call the owner to return the wallet. The man said that no one can be trusted anymore and they turned around without even saying thank you. To be honest I wanted to say Drop Dead to these ungrateful snobs but I simply said that they should enjoy their vacation. They drove away and rather than getting mad I simply told myself that I did the right thing by returning the wallet. I hope that they enjoyed their vacation but with the attitude that they displayed in front of me I highly doubt it.

2013-Savers ($85 Find)

In March of 2013 Barbara, our daughter-in-law Maria, and our one and only and favorite granddaughter Maya visited one of Barbara's favorite resale stores in Warwick called Savers. This thrift store offers secondhand clothing, footwear, furniture, books, and household items.

To be quite honest I myself never wanted to shop there since I didn't feel right buying or wearing other people's clothing whether it be new or slightly used. After some good-natured cajoling by my wife, she convinced me to go with them that day. She said that we would go to one of my favorite restaurants for soup and salad after we were done shopping since she knew that I loved Olive Garden. I agreed and we drove over to the store.

As I walked in the store, I saw many different sections of knick-knacks, shoes, jackets, ties, golf clubs, and toys and decided to go see if they had any London Fog raincoats or the sort of outerwear that I was thinking of buying.

To my astonishment almost immediately I found a jacket that looked like my size and I tried it on. I put my hands in the pockets to see if anything was left behind and I pulled out what seemed to be a rolled-up wad of tissues. I took out the wad and it was actually cash that totaled eighty-five dollars.

I found Barbara who by this time had numerous items in her carriage and told her about my newfound wealth. I told her that I planned on returning the money to a cashier but then she told me that the cashiers would most likely keep the money as they would have no idea who the money belonged to.

Instead, I gave each of the ladies, Barbara and Maria, forty dollars to spend and I kept five dollars to buy a few hopefully lucky lottery tickets.

After shopping we did go over to Olive Garden and enjoyed our lunch. Believe it or not, since that day I do occasionally go shopping at Savers, and yes, I must admit I always look in the pockets of anything that I try on whether it be brand new or slightly used.

Splitting the Bill (2018)

Do you know what the above phrase means?
As I read the words it means one of two things. Either each person pays their own portion of the bill or each person pays half the total combined bill.

While this may seem fair to most people, I respectfully disagree. If I order a hamburger and a soda and my friend orders a steak and whiskey sour then why should I pay more than my share while my friend, who should actually be paying more, gets a break? My wife and I have decided the last few years to always order a separate check for both of us and let our friends do the same. Most people are fine with our request but some are not.

A few years back we went out for dinner with some longtime friends from Cranston who each ordered the most expensive dinner along with two alcoholic drinks. I ordered a salad with chicken on the side and Barbara ordered a fish dinner. When the bill came, one friend said let's split the $140 bill. We spent approximately $40 and my friends' share was $100. So as not to create an incident and have tension with my friends I reluctantly opened my wallet, took out my credit card, and paid $70. You could almost see smoke coming out of the top of my head and I vowed then to always get my own separate check.

A few months after the incident above we went out with another couple who live in Massachusetts and I said to them that I wanted my own separate check. My friend's wife was appalled and asked me if we were mad and if we still wanted to be friends. She said no one had ever asked for a separate check in the many years that they had gone out for dinner. I explained why and they graciously understood my reasoning. I stuck to my request and asked the waitress for a separate check. Each and every time we go out to dinner since then I always ask for my own separate check. I also never order hors d'oeuvres or dessert. I never want to be in the position of having to discuss the bill for those items.

Over the years I have kept my receipts and I write the name of the restaurant, the initials of who we went out with, and what we had for dinner.

This way someday I may write another book entitled "Splitting the Bill."

Statue of Liberty (Follow-Up 2023)

In the summer of 1991, we were visiting our friends in New York and saw the Statue of Liberty. My friend's son almost fell off the base and I grabbed him to safety. (Read more about this in my book entitled *Right Place, Right Time* pages 93-95).

My friend promised to treat us all for dinner that night at a local Italian restaurant. I can't recall if he did. However, even thirty-two years later I would always remind my friend who now lives in Florida that he still owed me lunch or dinner. To this day he always tells me that he can't recall the story—or is it that he remembers but didn't want to pay for dinner?

Finally, he paid off his debt to me. This past October 9, 2023 my friend and his wife were on a cruise from their new home in Florida with some of their friends, with stops along the way which included Newport, Rhode Island. Barbara and I took the ferry from India Point in Providence and met them for a walk around Newport and of course lunch. I reminded my friend once again about his debt and this time, the heavens opened up. After we ate lunch, he took our bill and paid it in full. Love you guys (Ann and Mike Greenstein) from Florida.

Noises We All Hear and Ignore: From Birth to Death and Beyond

Noises that people hear. You may wonder why in the world I would have a short story in my book about noises. The answer is quite simple: I like how my fellow billion earthlings have always made and heard noises. Some are loud and some are quiet. Some are aggravating and some are not. My wife and granddaughter love to tell me that I eat too loudly and make unnecessary sounds and noises.

Many people may make noises that may aggravate people, but I highly doubt it.

The following is a listing of noises or actions that I have been known to do, not necessarily in any order. I like to call the list below "Trials and Tribulations of Living with Me and My Self-made Musical Notes and Tunes":

Slurping my soup
Sucking noises when sucking on hard candy
Farting, or as we like to say, tooting, in public
Pig oinking
Spitting in the sink or trash
Hocking up phlegm
Burping

Throwing coins in the water
Chewing my food loudly
Chewing gum and candy
Sniffing
Clearing throat
Hocking up loogies (nasal congestion)
And many more

Humans have five senses: vision, hearing, touch, smell, and taste. All of these senses are important in our daily lives.

You can probably guess that the most important sense for me is *hearing* after reading my short story.

As you can also probably surmise, all of the noises that I listed can be affected by any of the five senses.

All people make sounds at birth and at death.

It wasn't a wail, a burp, or an explosion from her diaper (did you begin to think that was all you'd ever hear from her?). The incredible sound you may have just heard is, in fact, a coo! There's nothing more adorable than a baby learning how to make her first sounds.

As someone approaches their demise or death, as it is commonly called, breathing patterns can change and secretions may collect in the throat. This can create a rattling noise known as the death rattle. It is part of the dying process. I personally have heard this noise numerous times in the past.

Why, you may ask, would I include a story about noises? The simple reason is that I wanted to. I have always been fascinated by sounds and noises and thought you might care about that, but probably not.

It's up to each and every one of us to determine what noises bother us sometimes or all the time.

I leave that up to you to decide.

Here's toot you.

STOLEN ITEMS

Delivering Bags of Furs (1975)

When I was twenty years old, I was in college living a good life. One day my now late brother asked me if I would take a ride with him to Mystic, Connecticut so he could meet a friend of his in a parking lot where a McDonald's is located today. I said sure and asked him what he was doing and who he was meeting. He told me he was doing a favor for a friend, his roommate at Providence College who lived in Connecticut. One Vito "Three Fingers" Centifanti. I am actually using a fake name for his roommate just in case he is still living, mainly because I don't want to end up sleeping with the fishes "if youse get my drift." I was afraid to ask him where the three fingers in his name came from; he said that it was best that I didn't know. I asked him why we had a large trash bag in the trunk and he said it wasn't my concern and don't ask him again. At the time I didn't think much of it but did find it rather odd.

On the drive to Connecticut my brother told me that I was to stay in the car and not say a word to whom he was going to be meeting. I asked him why and he told me to keep my mouth shut and he would give me $500. During this time in my life I was a college student, so an extra $500 in cash was good for me so I agreed to keep quiet and not ask any more questions. In less than an hour we got to Connecticut and my brother parked his car. He got out of the car and opened the truck and took out the large trash bag. He handed the bag to someone who I presumed was his roommate but to be honest I didn't pay too much attention and didn't try to get a look at his face. The man handed him an envelope and he then drove away. My brother got back in the car and we immediately got on Route 95 for the ride home.

A short time later my brother stopped at an exit and we got coffee and some snacks to munch on. I asked my brother what was in the envelope and he told me it was $10,000 in cash. He gave me my $500 and told me not to repeat the story to anyone else. He told me that his friend's dad was "connected" if you know what I mean. He said that it was just a simple business transaction. My brother repeated to me that I should mind my own business and not discuss it again.

Over the years my brother would occasionally drop a few names and tell me some stories about some of his "friends of mine."

You may wonder what he meant. I did as well until he explained the difference between "friend of Ours" and "friend of Mine" which were related to organized crime. Introductions were very particularly laid out. People not of the Mafia were introduced as "a friend of mine." Members were referred to as "a friend of ours."

When my brother said a few times that I shouldn't have any involvement or I could end up sleeping with the fish or have cement shoes put on, I knew what he meant.

And now "youse" know the rest of the story.

Missing Fishing Rod (1975)

When I was between the ages of five and twelve years old, my dad would take me and my two brothers fishing in Narragansett. We loved spending time with Dad. He had a nice fishing rod which he used to call a tuna rod. I loved using that fishing rod when he would let me. Many times, my father would promise that someday he would give me his fishing rod because I was the one out of three brothers who behaved most of the time when we were young. At the time we had inexpensive rods since, as we all know, young children fool around and break things and occasionally throw fishing rods off the dock into the water to see if they could float.

My father passed away in 1968. After his death the fishing rod stayed in our garage on Summit Avenue until we moved to Woodbury

Street on Providence's East Side a year or so later. Since I was twelve years old at the time my fishing career stopped as my other two uncles were busy raising their families and didn't have time to take us.

Years would go by and occasionally I'd see the fishing rod in the garage getting dusty, but I knew someday when I was older, I would take the fishing rod with me as my dad promised.

When I began to think about it one day when I was around the age of twenty or so I went looking for the fishing rod and noticed it was missing from the garage. I found out later that my older brother took the fishing rod with him when he moved to his apartment and then later to his house in Warwick, Rhode Island after he was married.

I used to ask him frequently about the fishing rod and said I wanted it because my father promised it to me. However, my brother said that I wouldn't ever get it and it didn't matter what my father had promised. He never disputed that fact, that he knew the fishing rod should be mine. Over many years I would always say to my brother when we spoke (which was infrequent) that he should return the fishing rod and he refused to give it back to me. Unfortunately, that was the type of person he was. Many years went by and I have no knowledge of the fishing rod's location. My brother passed away on February 11, 2024 at the age of sixty-nine from a heart attack and complications related to a lifelong battle with diabetes.

Since I'd had few conversations with my brother over the years and I also had nothing to do with his first ex-wife or his two children, or the daughter he had with his second wife who was then deceased, I contacted the attorney for his estate and asked about the fishing rod. He told me he would contact the beneficiaries of the estate. He said that he would ask them but it was their decision whether they would return the fishing rod. I've heard nothing from them since February 2024 so I assume the fishing rod is gone.

During this process I spoke to my younger sister who would tell us many times that she had been to my brother's house and I asked her about the fishing rod. Apparently, she was mad at us for some unknown

reason and when I asked about the fishing rod that my dad had promised to me, she told me that I could go dumpster diving for it or go to Savers and look to see if someone had dropped it off.

They were very hurtful comments and I don't know if I'll ever be able to forgive her. So, to this day all I have is a picture of my father with his fishing rod which I cherish. Perhaps someday the fishing rod will show up, which I doubt. It was one of the last good memories that I had with my dad and for some reason unbeknownst to me someone is holding onto the rod.

Anytime I go fishing with my own equipment now, I always think back to the days that my father took me fishing with his prize tuna rod that should be in my possession now but I realize never will be. It's only in my mind, in my memories and in my heart. Rest in peace Dad wherever you are. I love you and miss you.

The Stolen Glove (From a Young Boy Until the Present Time)

This story involves longtime family friends and because of this incident as well as other reasons we have nothing to do with them anymore, which is no great loss. When I was very young my dad would take me and my two brothers to play baseball in various places around the East Side in Providence, Rhode Island. I remember vividly that my father gave me a glove which I cherished from about age five until I was much older.

After my baseball days were over, I kept the glove in my home until I had children of my own and could go play baseball with them. Many years went by and my good friends had two children of their own. One day the mom, who we were very friendly with at the time, asked me if I had an extra glove that their son could use. Of course, I said they could use my prize possession, but it had to be returned once they bought a glove for their son at the end of the season. They agreed to my condition if I lent them my glove. I took the baseball glove out of storage and cleaned it up and gave it to the youngster to enjoy for the season.

At the end of the season, I asked for my glove back and was told that they could not find it. I asked them to look and they said they would. They told me numerous times they looked and could not find it and never even offered to replace it. This glove was a personal connection to my father and something I would miss.

Many years went by and I would occasionally ask our ex-friends about the glove and they would say to me that they could not find it and that was it.

About 2020 or a little before my ex-friends were moving down south, I contacted them and asked about the glove one more time. Since I knew they were moving and they would be emptying the house and packing boxes for their trip, I asked them again to try and find the glove. I heard nothing back from them at all and they did not even respond as to whether or not they looked for the glove. After they moved a few weeks later I emailed them again and asked about the glove. I never heard back. I did tell them that they never had the decency to tell me if they looked for the glove and they could have bought me a replacement. There's been no contact with them since and there never will be. I guess I learned a valuable lesson with my baseball glove: Never lend anything to anybody that you want returned, whether it be to a relative or a friend.

One of the most upsetting parts of the story is that my friend's wife had a very old camera in her possession that was her dad's before he died. She kept it in the garage for some unknown reason and when my son Max was taking some photography classes they asked if he wanted to borrow the camera. He said yes and I told Max as well as our ex-family friends that whenever they wanted the camera returned it would be returned.

Shortly after Max passed away in 2004, I was asked by the wife about the camera. I immediately told her I had it. Before we returned it, I cleaned the case and the camera. In short, I returned it exactly how it was when it was lent to us.

My ex-friend said she was happy that we returned something that was her father's possession. When I mentioned the glove that they never returned she said that it's only a glove. I told her it's not only a glove but a personal connection to my father, to which I received no response.

I guess someday when I leave this earth, I hope to see my father and spend time with him fishing and playing baseball in the afterlife if that truly does exist. I hold no malice or grudge against my ex-friends but I will never talk to them again in this lifetime.

Rest in peace Dad wherever you are. If there's an afterlife, then I hope you're playing baseball and fishing and thinking about me as I think about you every day.

STUPID AND DUMB INCIDENTS

Handbag Robbery Thayer Street (1970)

When I was around fifteen years old my friends and I would spend a lot of time riding our bikes up and down Elmgrove Ave to Wayland Square. We also spent many afternoons on Thayer Street which is the main street for restaurants and shops that cater to the students at Brown University in Providence, Rhode Island. We would lock up our bikes and then get something to eat.

On one of these occasions, we were walking near the bus tunnel that leads to downtown Providence. One of our friends, who happened to come from a wealthy family, said that he was planning on robbing an innocent person that day for no apparent reason. I told him he was insane and that he better not do anything like that. At that point I went to get my bicycle and decided to leave the area because I thought he might do it anyways since he was sometimes prone to irrational behavior.

As I started riding away, the next thing I heard was screaming. John (the name used for this story) indeed did attempt to yank the pocketbook off a woman who was walking and knocked her to the ground. Out of nowhere a crowd of college students started chasing my friends and one of them said that the guy on the bicycle was involved, meaning me. They began to throw rocks and branches at me as I rode away as quick as I could. I screamed at them that I was not involved and at that point they left me alone and started chasing my four friends. I made it home and later that night I called John and he told me he did not know what he was doing and he had too much to drink that morning.

I guess he must have felt guilty because he told his father and his father called the family attorney and they went to the Providence police station to admit to his crime.

He was charged with robbery but since he was under eighteen his case was sent over to juvenile court instead of adult court where he could have received a lengthy sentence and ended up in prison. At this point the judge told him he would be sentenced to probation for five years and highly recommended that he enter a program for people with alcohol and substance abuse issues. The judge told him that if he ever saw him in his courtroom again, he would send him to prison.

I decided after this incident that I would never have anything to do with at least these four guys because they were always in trouble. I always knew something like this would happen because friends of mine who had money always would do things arrogantly and stupidly thinking that their parents could get them out of trouble because they had political connections.

Out of all those friends most of them straightened out, and believe it or not John became a child psychiatrist, many years later practicing in Rhode Island.

I heard that he specializes in juveniles with aggression, ADD, and bad behaviors and is successful in treating them. I guess you could say of the end of the story is that crime never pays but going down the right path does, like it did with John in his later years.

Just one more tidbit on the story. It turned out that John's father, when he was running for United States Senate a few years later, just happened to hire the woman that his son robbed. She worked on his election campaign even though he lost his bid for the Senate.

Life does have more twist and turns than people realize but I guess things work like they are supposed to work, no more and no less. And as the late Paul Harvey used to say, "Now you know the rest of the story."

Shooting at Building (1971)

Back in 1971 through 1973 I was a pretty wild kid. I hung around with five or six "friends," some of whom had incidents with the police on numerous occasions. It was likely that most of my troubles were from hanging around with these idiots doing stupid things, but not ever enough to get arrested. Most of my friends came from educated and fairly upper-class families as I did, so we all should have known better. I came from a good family with both parents.

One friend now is a child psychiatrist and came from a very wealthy family; his father ran for the United States Senate numerous years ago.

Another friend who now lives down south had a dad who was a renowned heart surgeon.

Another friend's dad was a well-known attorney. This friend I see now and then and he works in a law firm today.

Another friend came from a fairly religious family but the son (my friend) was in and out of trouble since he was very rebellious. He spent some time in prison after his father died but I have heard through the grapevine that he finally settled down and no longer gets in trouble with the law.

My final friend and fellow gang member came from a wealthy family. This guy ending up starting a telephone company specializing in schools and hospital buildings. He became wealthy in his own right and has since retired and moved out of state.

I guess having money can give you privilege but not common sense or decency.

To protect myself and others, I will not give you the names of people or places involved in the following incident.

One time a few friends invited me to take a ride in their car and do some target practice. We had done this before with BB guns, shooting at targets in the woods, but never caused any damage to people or things. They initially told me they were going to set up some cans and shoot them in the woods in Providence.

When we arrived, just like in the movies, one of my friends opened up the back of his car and lifted up the blanket and underneath were rifles and shotguns. I didn't ask where they came from because I knew this guy had some "connections," so to speak, in the family, so he kept his business to himself and I kept quiet. I thought we would simply have some fun and that would be that.

They showed me how to load the guns and told me we could blast away at some of the abandoned buildings nearby. I thought it was like in the wild, wild west with us shooting what seemed like hundreds of rounds of ammunition. We blasted away, breaking windows in the buildings that were rundown and unoccupied. I did have the thought of if there was a security guy in the buildings. I sensed we were doing something wrong and I told my friends to stop immediately and put the guns back, then we left the scene and they took me home. I didn't really think anything about it except that we had fun, but we were really stupid and dumb for doing what we did.

The next day I was looking at the newspaper at my house and saw an article that said hundreds of shots were fired into a building the prior day and by chance the guy who roamed the property for security reasons had called in sick and no replacement took his job. I cut the article out of the paper and kept it in my wallet for many years, realizing what a stupid and ignorant thing I was involved in, and vowed never again.

We were lucky that the security guy wasn't at work that day; he could have been killed and I would not be here writing this story.

Well, the story and moral: If you're presented with something that seems stupid, walk away, no, run away and live for another day. And of course, when choosing friends choose them by their integrity, and not by their actions. This incident happened more than fifty years ago and to this day I still regret it.

UP, UP, AND AWAY

Flying with J.B. (1993)

In 1993 I was working with the US Department of Defense and I ran a government office at a defense contractor in Rhode Island that was manufacturing boats for the US Navy. Suffice to say I am not able to discuss the projects but if I ever did, I could lose my DD (Direct Deposit retiree check) and trade it in for an FPC (Federal Prison Cell). On a clear day in the spring or summer of 1993 I was outside on my daily noontime stroll when I noticed a fancy looking helicopter about to land on the helipad nearby. I waited until it landed and walked over and saw three gentlemen exit the chopper. One was the pilot and the other two were passengers. One of the men, a guy named J. B., asked me where the office of the defense contractor that I was working at was. I asked him what he was doing and he indicated that his company was in negotiations to buy numerous contractor facilities that manufactured high-end sailboats and expensive powerboats. While walking towards the office he asked me if I wanted to take a ride on the helicopter but I told him that I would need permission from the JAG (Judge Advocate General), also known as the government military attorney.

One of the two passengers I met that day was a CFO (Chief Financial Officer) of the largest company in the world with over two million employees, and the other was a senior executive there and a brother in the family that owns and controls it. The brother was the previously mentioned J. B. I won't go any further but will leave you with a small tidbit. The stock of that publicly traded company was less than three dollars a share then and today it trades at over fifty dollars a share. A $10K investment back then would be worth a lot of money today without ever selling, just investing the dividends and letting the value grow and grow.

J. B. told me that he was to be in Rhode Island for a few more days and he gave me his business card. I told him that I would let him know in the next few days if I could take a helicopter ride. I contacted the JAG and he told me that as long as I didn't discuss any US government business and took a ride on my own time and not work time then it wasn't prohibited. I called J. B. and told him I was available to meet on Saturday morning and we agreed that 9:00 a.m. would be fine. I was very excited and nervous at the same time, although I had been on a few military helicopters before this incident. We met on Saturday morning and the pilot, along with the two passengers and me, took off and we flew around Newport and many other locations.

While I was enjoying the scenery the two men were discussing all types of strategies and multimillion-dollar stock purchases, along with the names of companies that they were planning on purchasing in the United States and a few third world countries. I listened intently and I assume that they knew I heard what they were saying. I had never heard the term "insider trading" but we all know now. It means trading in a public company's stock or other securities by someone with non-public information about the company. I kept listening and decided that if I were to invest in these companies, I might be committing a serious felony and land in the "Big House," also known as the slammer.

After an hour or so we landed and I was asked to accompany both businessmen to a lunch at an exclusive restaurant in the Newport, Rhode Island area. We had a nice time and while dining I was asked what my background was. When I told them I had a degree in accounting and psychology the CFO said he wanted me to come work for him as a junior level executive. He offered me a rather hefty salary if I were to relocate to Arkansas and an enticement of a large amount of stock options that could be sold no earlier than five years after I started with the company. I told them I would discuss this at home and make a decision in the next few days. My family decided that since we had a young son at home, it wasn't the right time to relocate.

I contacted the CFO the following week and politely declined the offer. I never regretted my decision except to think that the stock options I would have received would have been worth many, many (did I say many?) millions of dollars in the years to come. Do I have regrets? Perhaps, but I will leave it up to the reader to decide if I ever purchased any stocks in those companies that were purchased south of the border. I will, however, say that I began to read the *Wall Street Journal* every day and if I saw any news about this company, I would occasionally make some investments as now this information was being discussed publicly and not considered insider trading.

In the ensuing years I kept in touch with the executives and was sad to hear that one of them passed away a few years later in 1995. I still have the business card of the CFO and over the years I spoke to him from time to time for some advice. One of the most important pieces of advice he gave me was to always live within or below one's means. He told me that most wealthy people live next door to ordinary people, don't buy expensive houses or cars, and never ever show or brag about their wealth. The final words of wisdom imparted on me were "that one never knows the path in life, whether it be right or left, but make your decision and never ever regret it and never look back." It's how I live my life now and always will.

Test Flight on Apache Helicopter Vomiting (1999)

During my career with the United States Department of Defense (DOD) I had many interesting experiences. The following story is about me taking a test flight on an Apache attack helicopter.

On many occasions I flew out to military bases or contractors all around the United States to participate in various activities and/or to be part of a team reviewing various military related items. One such time I flew to upstate New York to be part of a government team that was reviewing and analyzing the wiring harness of the Apache attack helicopter. The wiring harness controls all of the components of the aircraft and is essential to the operating and drivability of the helicopters.

The following is a brief history to give the reader a little knowledge of the helicopter: The AH-64 Apache is an attack helicopter that first flew in 1975 and is still manufactured today. It was designed by Hughes Helicopters, which later became McDonnell Douglas, which later became Boeing. The Apache has seen action in multiple conflicts worldwide and one costs approximately $50 million to build.

As a part of the review team, I was invited to take a test flight on the helicopter. I was asked to fill out a few forms which essentially said if I died while on a test flight, I was unable to sue the contractor. I was told that I could sue the government, but more likely, I could simply bend over and kiss my ass goodbye before I died. Was I scared shitless about this flight? You bet your ass! I'm sure you, the reader, would be as well.

After a few simple instructions I put on my flight suit and was given one simple instruction: If I felt like vomiting, I would be given a puke bag. The pilot named Commander "Viper" Jackson had flown many times before and told me if I puked on him, he would throw me out of the aircraft as it cruised along at a maximum speed of 182 mph. He was called "Viper" for a reason. He would kill you in a heartbeat, but I leave that story for another time.

We took off and he immediately started doing some very unsettling maneuvers, making my stomach flip-flop. I felt like heaving and bringing up my breakfast if you understand my meaning. We flew up and down along the valleys in upstate New York, and to be quite honest there was some beautiful scenery, at least what I could see of it. I was concentrating more on not vomiting or passing out.

The pilot spoke to me about his experience as a pilot and told me that you get used to the ups and downs, the sideways sweeps and deep diving of the helicopter, and that most pilots get queasy at first but get better. He had flown over five hundred missions during his military career; had suffered a few crashes and was scared shitless many times. He also sadly told me how numerous fellow pilots were killed by crashes or being shot down during battles.

I asked him how he and other pilots survived wartime conditions, and his response was training and faith and belief in a higher power.

That short two-hour flight taught me a lot about life. Life is what you make of it.

Belief in G-d or some higher power is probably all you need except faith.

I only flew in the Apache one time but believe me, the United States has the best educated and trained pilots in the world.

With more conflicts worldwide today I'm sure we will see many more Apache helicopters flying around doing what they do best: keeping Americans out of harm's way.

No matter what your political beliefs, whether it be Democrat, Independent, or Republican, just remember there are men and women in uniforms of all kinds who are doing their best every day to protect us by fighting for our freedom. G-d Bless America and always remember to G-d bless our troops. Amen.

Parachute with Max (August 11, 2002)

As many of the readers know, my son Max Gold Dwares was diagnosed with chronic myelogenous leukemia on March 8, 2001 and passed away at the young age of twenty on February 18, 2004. On August 11, 2002, I kept a promise that I had made to Max the day before his bone marrow transplant at the New England Medical Center in Boston. This procedure was to cure him of cancer. Max had spent the week prior to his BMT on July 27, 2001, reading and preparing for his life-altering procedure. He also looked out the window constantly as he was taking pictures of the Boston skyline, and we would see planes taking off and landing at Boston's Logan Airport every thirty seconds or so. It is one of the busiest airports in the world.

Max looked me in the eye that day and asked me to promise if, one year after his BMT he was alive and well, I would take him skydiving. It was a dream of Max's, and he felt it would be a way for him to get closer to G-d. I asked him if he was nuts but decided to say okay. He asked me to swear on my late father's soul that I would take him skydiving, and I said yes, assuming that Max would forget and not ask in the future.

On August 10, 2002, Barbara and Jake were visiting our good friends Ann and Mike Greenstein in Florida. I contacted Ann a few days prior and asked her to invite Barbara and Jake to come down to Florida for a visit. Without telling anyone, I also contacted a skydiving school in Rhode Island to make plans for Max and I to jump out of a perfectly good airplane. A day later Max and I went out for breakfast to George's in Cranston for bacon and eggs. While eating, Max looked me in the eye and asked me the question that I had put out of my mind over a year ago: "Dad, when are we going to skydive?"

"Whenever you're ready, Max," I said, assuming that he would chicken out.

"Now," he responded.

"Are you sure?"

He asked if I was afraid, and of course I said no, but I was scared shitless. No, let's say I was petrified. We planned on going for the jump the next morning, but I went to bed, hoping that Max would change his mind.

The morning came, and Max woke up bright and cheery, and I had a stomachache that wouldn't stop. What the hell was I thinking jumping out of a perfectly good airplane in the sky? Was I an idiot, and what if something happened to either Max or myself? Did we put Max through hell so he could then be injured or die from a skydiving accident? And most importantly, what would Barbara say? I had to make a basic assumption that she would be furious with me. No, better yet, she would kill me. Nevertheless, I had made a promise that I would keep no matter what the consequences were.

Max and I got up, had a light breakfast, and took a ride to North Central Airport in Lincoln, Rhode Island. I forgot to mention that I had notified some friends to come and join us, and they were there cheering us on our adventure, especially the Redlich family.

The weather was calm at 11:30 a.m., and Max and I went into the office to sign up for a jump from a perfectly good airplane. The first thing they give you is an eight-page waiver form to read and sign and date. It stated things such as every possible item that could go wrong while skydiving, beginning with death to amputation, crash, burns, etc. Very pleasant thoughts for so early in the morning. Both Max and I laughed out loud while reading the form, and after Max signed the form, he looked at me and said, "Dad, if anything happens to us, Mom will kill us, so we better land safely."

We proceeded outside to take our brief lesson, which consisted of jumping off a picnic table and getting up. That was the extent of it. We waited our turn to take the tractor out to the launch area as we would be ready to board the plane in the next fifteen minutes or so. We arrived and met our jump partners, two English lads here for the summer to earn some money.

Max and I got into our jumpsuits and proceeded onto the plane. The plane itself looked like a boxcar with no seats. We ambled up the three-step ladder and took our positions inside. We then were strapped to our jump partners. As first-timers, we were doing tandem jumps, in which you have an experienced jumper hooked onto your back to guide you in case you panic or crap your pants or pass out.

I could see Max smirking with his boyish grin but also fear was spreading through him. He told me that he wanted to be the first to jump as he knew if I went first, he could opt out of jumping, and if he went first, I, being his dad, couldn't be a chickenshit and back out.

Soon, the plane was barreling down the runway, and in about twenty minutes or so, we were at twenty-five thousand feet and banking back toward the jump zone. We were to jump from thirteen thousand feet. We were nuts, but I'd made a promise to Max, and it's a promise that I would keep.

Pretty soon, Max and his jump partner were standing up and getting ready. The cameraman opened the door, and away he went. I was scared to say the least. Max looked over at me and gave me a thumbs-up, and he went toward the door. The lights went, red, yellow, and green, and out he went. Three, two, and one, and out the door he went into the hands of G-d. What was I thinking? What if something happened to Max, and he died that day? I would have to retrieve his body and tell his mother.

I said a quick prayer, and it was my time to get up. My turn was fast approaching. Within two minutes or so, it was my turn to go toward the door. I was scared and thought about backing out, but I couldn't. If my son could jump, so could I.

We stood up, and in a few seconds, we were barreling toward the ground at an incredible rate of speed. We then began to float like a butterfly for what seemed an eternity. I could not see much from thirteen thousand feet but silently said a prayer to G-d to take care of Max and deliver him from all of the pain that he was in. I hoped that G-d would be listening. The ride down from the heavens back to earth was actually quite peaceful. It seemed like an eternity but actually lasted approximately seven minutes. It was a thrilling experience, and I was glad to touch the ground.

Even though Max jumped before me, I landed first due to the weight differences between us. I unhooked my chute and waited for Max to land. A few seconds later, out of the sky came Max like an angel floating down from heaven. He landed, looked pooped, gave me a hug and kisses, and ran to the bathroom. He later told me that although he loved the thrill, he was scared to death and was thankful that he was able to be close to G-d for a brief few moments. When I asked him what he said to G-d on his journey from the heavens to the earth, he responded that it was between him and his Maker. We went home shortly thereafter and took a long nap, as we were exhausted.

I kept my promise to my son and even though I got some flak from family members and many friends that thought I was too reckless and Max or myself could have been hurt, I never once have regretted my decision. If Max were still here on earth, I would take him skydiving again in a heartbeat.

(Feel free to read more about Max's life in the book that Max and I cowrote entitled *Live to the Max*. It's a true story about Max's faith and belief in G-d and mankind while battling leukemia.)

Max: I love you and miss you. I hope that you are resting in peace. I think of you often and realize that the time that you left us seems to have gone by very quickly. I have heard many people say that time heals the loss. I don't actually believe any of that bullshit. The only thing I know is that you are not here, so to me it's simply a "new normal" in our lives while you are not here with us. I can't wait to see you again in the future, "soon" but "not too soon." *L'chaim*.

ABOVE: Kevin Dwares shows a scrapbook he kept on the life of his son Max and "Live to the Max," the book he finished after Max died of bone cancer in 2004, at age 20.
LEFT: Max Dwares skydiving, which was in keeping with his philosophy of life, summed up in a quote from the movie "The Shawshank Redemption": "Get busy living or get busy dying."

THE PROVIDENCE JOURNAL
PHOTOS/BOB BREIDENBACH

WORLD PROBLEMS OR JUST EVERYDAY ISSUES

What do I mean by first world problems? It means a simple problem, at least compared to the serious problems facing those in the developing world.

While my final three short stories below are mine, they may relate to others as well. During my family's time in our first apartment and later in our two homes we had a lot of good times and some stressful times. In each of our residences we experienced some problems with Freon leaks and other issues. I hope that you enjoy the stories that follow and can relate to some if not all of them.

Irving Avenue Stories (1980-1985)–Our First Apartment

When Barbara and I were first married we rented an apartment at 154 Irving Avenue off Blackstone Boulevard on the East Side. We lived there from 1980 to 1985 until we bought our first house in the Stadium section of Cranston. My first experience with first world problems begins with my refrigerator experiencing a Freon leak. First let me give a brief history of Freon.

Freon is a brand of refrigerant that was once used in refrigerators to cool food and keep it at the proper temperature. It is no longer used since it is considered toxic. One way to see if your refrigerator is having a leak is to look for a frost or ice buildup.

In 1984, a few years or so after we moved into our apartment, we began to notice heavy ice buildup in our freezer. At the time our freezer wasn't a frost-free item since our landlord supplied the least expensive appliances. I contacted him many times and told him about the ice and his response was to simply empty it and put a pan of water in the freezer to melt the ice. Well after the third or fourth time I decided to get a hammer and a very large ice pick and I began to pound away and chop at the ice. Barbara was insistent that I not use the ice pick but of course I didn't listen. A few minutes later I began to smell a very unusual smell, and after calling a few appliance stores it was determined that I must have punctured something inside the freezer thereby releasing Freon gas. I called the landlord and told him that the fridge stopped working. Of course, I didn't tell him about the hammer and ice pick.

I told him that both Barbara and I were getting a headache and Max age one was acting very agitated.

The landlord was mad that the fridge died but he was insistent that we leave the apartment immediately since he suspected the unit was leaking Freon. He promised that a new appliance would be delivered by the end of the day. It was delivered later that afternoon and set up in the kitchen. The landlord asked me about the holes in the freezer and I simply said I had no idea. He smirked at me but said nothing. I am sure he knew what I had done but he looked at our one-year-old son Max and probably felt bad for us. Either way I thanked him for his kindness.

In mid-1984 I experienced another incident that may seem too far-fetched to have occurred, but the top of my head knows the truth.

I saw an advertisement on television for a set of forty-watt light bulbs for twenty dollars from the Association of the Blind. Since we always used light bulbs, I figured it was a good idea to buy some extra ones and help out a charity. I purchased them and a week or so later they arrived in the mail. I was happy to have them and also do a good deed. The next morning I screwed one into the overhead fixture. My usual method was to screw in the light bulb and turn my face away when I flipped the switch or pulled the chain. As soon as I pulled the chain the light bulb exploded, showering glass on top of my head. I called out to Barbara and she immediately came to help me. She gently used a brush to get the glass pieces out of my hair before I showered.

The next day I contacted the company to explain what happened and the technician asked me to send them any of the glass pieces from the bulb and the base. I asked her how I was supposed to get it out of the socket and she explained that I was supposed to take a potato and jam it into the socket and twist it out, which I did. I sent everything to them in the prepaid package. They explained they needed to determine if the glass imploded from the inside or from the outside. This would determine if there was a manufacturing defect or not. A few weeks later they sent me a check for $900 for my aggravation and explained that it was indeed a defect in the process when they were made. I contacted them and said I will not accept the check and I'm going to return it. They said to keep it or donate it to a charitable organization. I then decided to give it to the American Cancer Society and at that point the issue was closed.

Sometime in early 1984 I had built a bookcase and attached it to the wall in our living room next to a couch. I thought I'd done a good job but as you read the rest of the story, you'll realize I did not. We had asked the landlord if we could take some of the wallpaper down and replace it at our expense, to which he agreed. After removing some of the wallpaper we noticed the base of a fixture on either side of the wall. I didn't know what they were but later learned that they were called sconces. A sconce is a light fixture mounted on a wall, usually attached with a decorative base. I didn't give it much thought but I decided to see what was inside.

I should have used a flashlight but instead I just took a screwdriver and touched the inside. The next thing I knew I woke up coughing blood. My wife told me that she was watching me touch the fixture when I hit an electric wire and blew myself across the couch like Superman (or super idiot) and my back slammed into the bookcase which tumbled down upon me. I felt woozy for a short time. Barbara called the doctor and he said that if I didn't cough up any more blood, then all would be well. He said if I had any more spitting up of blood then I should come in for an x-ray or checkup. Within an hour or two I felt much better. Luckily, I just had a minor bruise from the bookcase that landed on top of me. I never played the electrician role again and instead decided that if I ever needed any electrical or plumbing work I would only hire a professional, and that's the truth of my story.

Packard Street Stories 1985-2017– Our First Home

We purchased our first home in October 1985 in the Stadium section of Cranston, Rhode Island. A few weeks earlier Hurricane Gloria hit Rhode Island and did a considerable amount of damage. After closing with the attorneys from both sides we came over to our new house very excited. There was minimal damage to the house we just bought except for a fence section that blew down. While emptying boxes from the U-Haul that we rented and walking around our new house we noticed a few things right away. The antenna on the roof of the house was gone, as well as the electric garage door opener both on the inside and outside of the garage. A few days after we moved in, we had an electrician come over to do some small projects and when I mentioned that we were told at the inspection that the house had 100 amps in the electrical panel he said that it was actually only 60-amp service. I contacted my uncle who was our closing attorney and he said it wasn't worth pursuing the matter as it would cost more in legal fees than it was worth. We were upset but decided to forget about it and move on with our first house that we would raise our two sons in.

Now to continue with the next Freon issue. We had two refrigerators/freezers in our house; one in the kitchen and one in the basement. I thought I had learned my lesson way back in 1984 in our apartment when I used a hammer and ice pick to get rid of the ice that built up in the freezer, but as you read further on, apparently not.

In November 2003, the night before Jake's bar mitzvah, I did the same thing with the fridge. Ice was building up in the freezer so once again I took a hammer and ice pick to it with disastrous results. That same day I had to ask a few friends of mine to come over and help me drag it out of the basement and put it on the front lawn for the trash men to pick up the following week.

If I recall, since we were busy celebrating our son's religious ceremony, it took us a few weeks to replace the unit. Let me briefly explain to you what a bar mitzvah is.

A bar mitzvah is when a thirteen-year-old Jewish boy is considered a man in the Jewish religion. He can participate in opening the ark where the Torah scrolls (laws or teaching of Judaism) are kept and can have an Aliyah which means you're praying to God when the Torah is out.

We had planned on having a luncheon in Jake's honor at the temple. Any leftovers were going to be put in the basement fridge. By sheer luck we didn't have that much but we froze what we could in the upstairs appliance. I hoped after this incident I wouldn't be taking a hammer and ice pick to any refrigerator/freezer again. It wouldn't happen again, however in 2019, some sixteen years later, we had another Freon issue (see the March 2019 Balsam Court story).

A Few More Packard Street Stories

June of 2013: I was at work at the Naval War College in Newport, Rhode Island when I got a phone call from the police that my elderly neighbor was in my garage. I wondered what he meant and he then said that her car went through the side of my garage after she hit the gas pedal instead of the brake. The only thing keeping the garage in place was the cable wire that I set up connecting the house to the garage a few years prior when Jake was in high school. He put a couch in the garage to hang out with friends. It was also filled with furniture that we had been collecting for them when they were ready to move into a place of their own.

Everything in the garage was a total loss. The day the garage was ruined the electric company came and turned off the power and I contacted the insurance company. We were told to immediately hire a contractor to board up the windows and to order a dumpster. They also told me to take an inventory of everything in the garage. The adjuster said he was going on vacation for one week from that day and would be in touch. The next day the city inspector came to our house and deemed the garage a total loss due to the fact that cans of gasoline and paint had broken open, ruining everything inside. The adjuster told me to have the entire garage emptied as it was a potential fire hazard, and to take an inventory of all the items for insurance claims purposes. In the meantime, my insurance adjuster told me that I needed to put a claim against my neighbor's insurance (she admitted fault for hitting my garage).

At the last minute her insurance company said they would pay everything in full; for the garage to be taken down, for everything that was disposed of, and the building of a new garage. However, there was a glitch in the entire process when the contractor I hired to rebuild told me that I needed a new cement foundation eight inches off the ground, which was the current regulation, and he hoped that I had an unforeseen conditions clause in my home owner's insurance policy. I wasn't sure that I did until I read the policy and after I contacted my agent, he said that the $8,000 charge to put in a new foundation would be paid in full. In the end my insurance company paid the claim and subrogated against my neighbor's policy. We had a new garage and all the destroyed items were replaced.

That's the end of the Packard Street stories.

Balsam Court Stories (2017-Present) Our Second and Hopefully Final Home.

We moved into our new home in Garden City in Cranston in October 2017. We thoroughly loved the idea of living in a ranch style house with living and dining room and bedrooms, bathroom, and laundry room all on the main floor. Many people purchase a home and go about making some minor or major improvements to make it their own. The house that we bought had everything that we wanted:

Laundry room in first floor
Walk-in shower
Three bedrooms
Two bathrooms, one with a walk-in shower
Den
Gas fireplace
Deck
Attached garage
Three-season porch
Vinyl siding
Outdoor sprinkler system
Central air
Gas central heat

Over the next few months we decided to modernize and replaced some things to make the house ours.
We were busy taking care of the following items:

Replaced all ten porch windows
Replaced porch door
Replaced breezeway windows
Replaced breezeway door
Replaced all pressure treated boards on deck
Installed numerous sensor lights around house
Installed new garage door opener
Widened the driveway from single-sided to double-sided
Put louver blinds in the kitchen and on the breezeway
Installed a new gas hot air heating system
Installed new water heater with twelve-year warranty

Installed a new sump pump
Installed two new wooden floors in the back bedrooms
Updated and refinished all the other rooms
Painted several rooms
Repointed chimney and replaced the chimney crown
Added set tub (sink in basement)
Added a pump to empty set tub to go directly to sewer (This was updated in April 2024 when I had the cast-iron pipe replaced with PVC piping)
Installed brand new wall down in office located in the basement
Put in brand new fence around the backyard property
Replaced downspouts
Installed gutter guards
Replaced outside outlets on garage
Put new lights down at fire pit area
Put down slate tiles at five-foot area around the trash bins
Installed ceiling fans, two in the kitchen and one in the living room
Put awnings over back door, front door, and large window in front of house
Installed new water spigots, one in front of house and one on back deck

We finished all of our projects around early spring 2018 and I am glad we did and so was my wallet.

June 2018

In the summer of 2018 Barbara and I decided to have a get-together with family and friends at our house. We planned a cookout and bought everything needed, from drinks to burgers and dogs (not the barking type; just the cooking type) and desserts. A while after everyone arrived, I lit the Weber gas grill and let it preheat. My daughter-in-law Maria, my son Jake, and my granddaughter Maya arrived. A friend of ours who was having some trouble walking came over and asked if I could move my car up a little closer to my garage so she could park in the driveway and have fewer steps to walk into the house. I obliged and moved the car so it touched the garage and went back to my chef duties.

A few minutes later Maria asked me if she could borrow our cat carrier and I told her it was in the garage on the shelf in the back. At the time the button to open the garage door was on the breezeway wall. It didn't make any sense, since you couldn't see the garage door from the breezeway. A few minutes went by and I heard a few unusual sounds, like things breaking and metal twisting. Unbelievably when Maria (obviously not her fault) pushed the button to open the garage I didn't realize that the car was touching the garage. The handle of the garage door went up and hit the bumper. Parts of the garage door imploded and the garage door opener inside burnt out and needed to be replaced. We laughed about it even though I wasn't happy, but that's called owning a house and taking care of business.

March 2019

Now to get to the third Freon story of my life. In March 2019 Barbara told me there was a chemical smell coming from inside the refrigerator purchased by the prior owners of the house in 2005. It smelled like the Freon gas we experienced two other times. We called a few appliance stores as well as a few appliance technicians and they all agreed it must be a Freon leak. We decided to go to Home Depot and purchased a new unit with an extended five-year warranty that expired in March 2024. After a couple of minor issues that were covered under the warranty the refrigerator still is in its proper place in our kitchen.

May 2, 2023

In May of 2023 I began the yearly process of turning on my outdoor sprinkler system as I had done since we purchased our house in 2017. The sprinkler company was set to arrive the next day or so to test the system to make sure it was working properly, including checking the sprinkler heads. All I had to do was turn the outside spigot off, turn the inside sprinkler module on the test cycle, and then turn the water handle in the basement to feed water to the system. I turned the valve on and within a minute or so I saw water coming in the basement where the floor met the wall. I shut off the water and called the sprinkler company and they said they'd come the same day to investigate. They determined that the outside irrigation system had failed. The system includes the following items:

- Valve box: This is the underground part of the system
- Control valves: These control the flow of water through the system
- Timer: This controls the operation of the valves and when to turn them on or off
- Backflow preventer: This prevents water traveling from your lawn sprinklers back to the drinking water within your home
- Pressure regulators: These ensure consistent water pressure throughout the system, preventing issues like water hammer or uneven watering.

It was determined that since the system was between twenty and twenty-five years old most of the components had failed. The main cause, they believed, was the handle inside that turned the water supply off and on had failed and allowed small amounts of water to leak all year into the outside system. When I turned on the system inside all that water trapped outside bubbled to the surface and came into my basement. They said the immediate fix was to replace the valve going outside my house from the basement and also the entire system outside the house which included the spigot, the backflow preventer, and all the control boxes. The plumber came over first to replace the shutoff handle for the water. The next day the irrigation company came and replaced everything on the outside of my house that controlled the system. As of the writing of this story the system has been turned on for the season and I have had no problems bubbling up to the surface (pun intended).

Hot Water Heater Replacement
May 24, 2023

You may not believe this, but a few weeks after we had the irrigation system fixed, I noticed a small amount of water leaking underneath my hot water heater in the basement. The Rheem water heater was installed in October 2017 and it had a twelve-year warranty; it was only six years old. The plumber came over and told me the heater was history, dead as a door nail, or crapped the bed (so to speak) and he called the manufacturer and they said it was indeed under the warranty time frame. We drained the system and we brought it back to Home Depot where it was originally purchased. The warranty I found out was prorated and since the cost of the water heater had doubled since I purchased the original unit it still cost me more than the cost of the original unit. I bought it and brought it home and the plumber installed it.

 Well, I assume from reading these stories you may think that I am complaining about owning and maintaining a home. I am not. I am just telling you that things break down over time, like appliances and even people themselves. I am simply finalizing this chapter of stories but you may appreciate my French drain story in a prior chapter entitled "Lessons in Life." As the French people like to say, adieu. or bye-bye for now.

WORLD PROBLEMS— AT LEAST IN MY OWN MIND

Tomato "Capers" (Ongoing)

My short story is about my allergy to all tomato products and I want to share some of my encounters with you very briefly. I am not talking about "capers" but you will soon understand what I am babbling about.

You may think I mean a goofy little joke or prank, a crime or a ridiculous adventure.

Over numerous years, I have developed a sensitivity to tomato and tomato-related products but no one seems to take it seriously. Most times when we go out to a restaurant and I tell the waiter or waitress about my allergy they don't seem to believe me.

A tomato allergy can cause a variety of symptoms such as skin rash, hives, and shortness of breath, among other serious problems.

The following incidents happened at various restaurants that put tomatoes or tomato products in food that I ordered even after me telling the waiter/waitress many times that I have a severe tomato allergy. I will briefly list a few of the incidents below:

1. Ordered salmon and it came to the table with rings of tomatoes all around it. The waitress said "I didn't think you'd have an issue with them as long as you ate the fish that wasn't touched by the tomatoes."
2. Ordered a hamburger and there was a small container of ketchup on the plate. When I mentioned it to the waitress her response was she put the order in, but she didn't bring it to the table.

3. Ordered chicken fajitas at a local restaurant and told them about my allergy. Ate the dinner and within a few minutes had a terrible stomachache. I called the restaurant and when I asked if they used any tomatoes products the response was "Only in the rice do we put tomatoes, onions, celery, bell peppers, and tomato juice." (What a bunch of idiots.)
4. Went to a restaurant that specialized in fish and there were tomato chunks all over the fish.
5. Went to a well-known chain restaurant. I ordered chicken and on top of it were a few large pieces of tomato. The manager apologized and said that I could get anything else on the house. I ordered soup and salad and after taking only one spoonful I knew immediately that there were tomatoes in the soup. He went into the kitchen and was told that the soup came into the restaurant in large bags with no list of ingredients.

I will conclude my discussion about tomato allergies and include a short story about my good friends, Steve and Ronnie Sirota, and our experience at a local restaurant that specializes in Italian food which often has tomato sauce served with the pasta, chicken parmigiana, and many other fine dishes. I would like to say up front that Steve provided me written permission to use his full name for the short story and also allowed me to somewhat embellish the story but not as far as embarrassing him (maybe just a little).

I ordered my usual fish dish (without any tomato products) and Barbara ordered some type of chicken dish that she said was quite tasty. Steve's wife Ronnie ordered her dish which I recall may have also been a fish dish. When it was Steve's turn to order he told the waiter that he loved a very generous amount of tomato sauce on his dish, which included chicken and a very large serving of pasta. The waiter actually showed Steve the proper way to eat pasta with a spoon, which is customary in Italy and considered a classy way to eat. The night was very relaxing and we all enjoyed our food and our conversation as well.

An hour or so later as we were winding down our time together, the waiter came over and asked us if we wanted any boxes to take home any leftovers, of which there were plenty for all of us. I of course had my usual joke and told him that I would rather do judo versus boxing (if you get my corny joke). We all laughed a little, or should I say I was the only one who laughed at my silly comment. The waiter who was very friendly and professional said that it would be his pleasure to take the plates and put all the food in the Styrofoam container. Steve told him that he was quite capable of doing it himself. The waiter tried to tell Steve that since the dish he ordered was very saucy he should take care of it. Steve insisted that he could take care of this small mission all by himself.

Well now the story gets somewhat funny at least from where I was sitting, directly across from Steve. I tried to tell Steve that it would be better if the waiter boxed up the leftovers but Steve was very insistent. Steve spent most of his career in the financial services industry so he has a very analytical mind and makes decisions his way. He won't or can't let anyone tell him what to do, except perhaps his lovely wife Ronnie.

Steve lifted up his plate and started to slowly spoon the very saucy pasta (did I say saucy? You bet) into the Styrofoam box. Within five to ten seconds some of the saucy pasta fell from the spoon onto Steve's pants. He laughed a little but most likely was somewhat embarrassed and couldn't or wouldn't admit his small failure in front of his wife or his two friends. I must admit I was laughing inside but did my best to say calm and not say anything. The waiter came over when he saw what happened and tried to take over the process of boxing up the pasta, but Steve insisted it was his way and no other way at all. The waiter said that he should finish but once again Steve insisted he would complete the mission at hand.

Steve got up from the table and he could see that the tomato sauce had leaked somewhat onto his pants but at this moment was not too bad. He asked the waiter for some napkins but again insisted he would finish his mission.

Steve then sat down and asked the waiter for a plastic bag to put the Styrofoam container in when he finished putting in the remaining sauce. Well…that didn't end well. As Steve finished putting the pound or so of pasta drenched in tomato sauce into the container, he forgot to factor in that the pasta was quite heavy. Apparently it moved in the box and dramatically leaked out into the bag, which by then had sprung a "small" leak. At this stage the pasta sauce leaked like an oil geyser and ended up all over his pants. Steve seemed not to be upset but you know that he had to be somewhat embarrassed and refused to show it. We asked the waiter for the bill and the chitchatting was over.

When we left the restaurant Steve and Ronnie asked us if we wanted to come over for dessert. Being my usual funny self I said sure, as long as we weren't going to be eating pasta with sauce or anything else like it. We drove to Steve and Ronnie's house and Steve excused himself to change into some clean clothes. Steve's dog Jenny, a goldendoodle, saw Steve when we came into the house and initially ran up to give him a kiss, but I swear I saw a large grin on Jenny's face and she didn't even bother to kiss him. A few minutes went by and Steve came into the kitchen and told me that he put his sauce-stained pants into the washing machine to clean them. We laughed a little and Steve showed us a few of his collections from their travels around the world, which to be quite honest were very impressive. We left a short time later and I did text Steve to say that we had a great evening and that we would go out to dinner again in the future. The next day Steve called and said that his pants were ruined and he planned on buying a new pair in the next few days.

Since the sauce incident we have gone out with Steve and Ronnie but I believe we haven't yet returned to an Italian restaurant for pasta and sauce. Did Steve learn anything from the night he was drenched in pasta sauce? I assume not but as the saying goes, "Oil's well that end well." Yuk, yuk, yuk.

I assume after Steve reads this short story, we will still remain friends but will stay away from pasta dishes.

Rather than go on and on, at least ten additional times I have had similar incidents with tomato products on my dinner. I would like to also say that I have had numerous incidents in which my tomato allergies were handled appropriately.

A few local places we went out for dinner always took me seriously and did the right thing such as:

- Changing gloves when making my dinner
- Using a separate knife
- Using a separate pan/plate to prepare and present my dinner

Tomato allergies are not taken seriously, at least in my dining experiences. People seem to have a better understanding and appreciation for allergies that are more well-known, like allergy to chocolate, potatoes, strawberries, etc. I would hope that by reading my short stories about my allergy to tomatoes, people will talk about it and take it seriously.

THE SPELLING OF THE WORD G-D

You may wonder why throughout the book I spell the word G-d instead of the most common spelling with three letters. Some people of the Jewish faith believe that this is a sign of respect and comes from an interpretation of the commandment in Deuteronomy 12:4 regarding the erasing, destroying, or desecrating the name of G-d. Writing "G-d" instead of spelling out the three letters is a fairly recent custom in America. Many believe this to be a sign of respect. According to the medieval commentator, Rishi, we should not erase or destroy G-d's name and should avoid writing it. Some people of the Jewish faith will avoid discarding paper or books in which G-d's name appears in Hebrew. Rather than being thrown out or destroyed, they may be stored in a *genizah* (a storage place) and buried in a Jewish cemetery. Throughout my life I have always spelled the name G-d out of my own personal belief and respect.

MY FINAL THOUGHTS

This book that you are reading is a continuation of my prior book *Right Place, Right Time*. The fifty-seven additional short stories I believe end the stories that I have kept bottled up inside for over sixty-eight years. Telling them and writing them on paper have been a tremendous emotional release for me and I am glad that I finally got it done, although it took a lifetime of living.

Barbara has always told me that with all the deaths in my immediate family from my dad, uncle, son, brother, etc., I needed a therapist. I guess writing these books has been and always will be my therapy. Barbara has always told me that I should forgive and forget friends and relatives who I believe have transgressed against me. To be honest I have always had a hard time doing just that. Sometimes I blame myself for my son Max's death. I question myself if I did the right thing. Did I make the correct medical decisions or not? In reality everything we do and every decision that one makes is all in G-d's hands.

I do put a lot of unnecessary stress on myself by thinking about the world and how it should be. I have almost come to realize that there is very little if not nothing that I can change except for my own behavior. I can't change how others live or act in the world we live in.

The world that we are leaving to our children and grandchildren is all messed up in my own humble opinion. It's not too late to change if we all try to make the planet a better place to live.

It's very expensive to live today but it was the same years back and most likely throughout history. I have always lived within my means, and paid down my debt and invested wisely so the future would be brighter at least financially. Remember in the past there was no cable television and a family didn't have two or three cars in the driveway. We didn't go out to dinner and spend three hundred dollars as if that was normal. There was no Netflix, no HBO or Amazon TV. We didn't take cruises or spend $10,000 taking a family on a Disney vacation. We didn't spend ten dollars on a cup of Starbucks coffee and a muffin. People back then I believe were more conservative. Today a lot of people live for today and don't think of the future.

Today families need a double income just to survive. A lot of middle-class folks send their children to Ivy League schools that they can't afford simply for the prestige. Why not send your child to a trade school where you can make a damn good living? Some people protest but many don't get involved and would rather stay insulated in their own homes.

What has the world come to? Have we no shame or any regrets? Thinking or believing in a higher power like G-d seems to be a thing of the past.

More and more mankind is hurting their own health, with heart attacks and cancer dramatically on the rise. WHY? We are the wealthiest country in the world but the medical system in the US and most modern countries is an abysmal failure.

We have Republicans, Democrats, and Independents who are constantly arguing about their own opinions and it is creating wedges within society and most importantly within families. No one seems to respect the other side's opinion anymore. Maybe no one ever did. Social media in my humble opinion has ruined society to a degree not seen before in humankind. Life is moving too fast and not in a good way. Go into any restaurant and see a family of four which may include a set of parents and their two children. They are all on their phones. Wouldn't it be better if the family members all were talking to each other rather than pecking away on the phone keyboard sending out a multitude of texts that most times are probably useless? I am not inferring that every one of the phones is communicating unnecessarily but probably that is the case.

Are we out of our minds?! Let's get back to some sense of normalcy. Let's put G-d back into the world. Let's put human decency and kindness back into the world. Why can't people respect one another no matter what religion, race, color, creed, or social status level? Why are we more and more being controlled by the people who live in castles and by dictators worldwide? We need to stop and smell the coffee and the roses and get back to the beginning of our existence. It was a much harder life back then but I believe mankind was happier than they are today.

Modern technology has ruined us. Why not lock up the devices we all have such as cell phones, minimize the use of them and spend more time with each other? Communication is supposed to be just that. People using their words and not using their fingers to tap out hundreds of nonsensical text messages all day long.

I had attempted to write a summary of my life and the way that I have lived. But in the end, I decided that my short stories told it all. In conclusion I simply say, thank you for reading my book. I told the truth and perhaps someday the reader may also choose to put pen to paper. None of us know when the clock of life will run out for all of us. So, for me, the present seemed the correct time and place to tell my stories.

Many of the fifty-seven short stories that I wrote also had a direct impact on some of my boyhood friends. I have not consulted with any of them about telling the stories but if they may read the book, they will know who they are. They need not worry since nowhere in my book have I used any real names, or exact time frames. I am also certain that since many of my stories occurred over fifty years ago the statute of limitations has long since expired. Some of my friends that had participated in some of my stories have been deceased for some time. I would, however, say that many years back I did contact some of the unintended victims and profusely apologized for many immature, dangerous, and thoughtless actions, and I even was graciously given a thank-you for my apologies. I am not rehashing any stories in my book to ask for total forgiveness or absolution. I am simply telling the truth and writing this book has allowed me to empty my heart and mind of years of things bottled up inside, allowing me to finally have some peace and tranquility for my heart, mind, and soul.

I had thought about including numerous other stories but decided that the behavior was simply too egregious for anyone to understand or accept and decided it was best to exclude them.

Finally, I always wonder why we mourn people who pass away before us. The people who left are no longer in physical or mental pain. From what I have read, people who die feel no pain or regrets. Wherever they end up, whether it be heaven, hell, purgatory or none of those, they are at peace. Perhaps the deceased mourn us. We are sad that we have lost friends and relatives, and some of us (not me directly) can never get past the loss of a loved one. I personally believe that time always marches forward. Loss is just a new normal of living, so I intend to always live life to the fullest and of course live to the Max.

I will leave the reader with the following poems. This first one is by Marianne Baum, a Jewish activist executed during WWII.

> Every minute someone leaves this world behind.
> Age has nothing to do with it
> We are all in "the line" without knowing it.
> We never know how many people are before us.
> We cannot move to the back of the line.
> We cannot step out of the line.
> We cannot avoid the line.
> So, while we wait in line -
> Make moments count.
> Make priorities.
> Make the time.
> Make your gifts known.
> Make a nobody feel like a somebody.
> Make your voice heard.
> Make the small things big.
> Make someone smile.
> Make the change.
> Make love.

Make up.
Make peace.
Make sure to tell your people they are loved.
Make sure to have no regrets.
Make sure you are ready.

This second poem…I have no idea who wrote it and the internet is less than helpful, but I agree with its message.

Dare to Dream
(No Known Author)

You work 8 hours to live 4.
You work 6 days to enjoy 1.
You work 8 hours to eat in 15 minutes.
You work 8 hours to sleep 5.
You work all year just to take a week or two vacation.
You work all your life to retire in old age.
And contemplate only your last breaths.
Eventually you realize that life is nothing but a parody of yourself practicing your own oblivion.
We have become so accustomed to material and social slavery that we no longer see the chains…

Remember that Life is a gift.
Get busy *living* or get busy *dying*

And always remember to *Live Life to the MAX*

WHAT THE TRUTH MEANS WHEN TELLING STORIES "RIGHT PLACE, RIGHT TIME"

It simply means to tell your version of events as accurately as possible. Keep it short, keep it sweet, and don't repeat. Only the writer knows the events and how they occurred. Speak from your heart and soul plainly.

Truth to me means the actual state of a matter, an adherence to reality or an indisputable fact. Truth refers to the version of reality that we exist in. Truth simply implies widely accepted facts which do not change over period, circumstance, or location. These are reality and accepted with no doubt.

I hope that you have enjoyed my saga of *Right Place, Right Time Part 2*. Some of you probably thought I made up some if not all of the short stories. I know that some of you may have found my stories funny, entertaining, and somewhat laughable. Well, that was the point.

Some of you may have not liked my saga at all. That is of course your prerogative.

For those of you who felt that my personal experiences helped you to perhaps be able to articulate your own feelings, I am grateful and humbled that my words may have helped a little bit. While discussing some of my stories with some friends and relatives, some began to tell me some of their own real-life incidents but were not ready to share them.

I leave you with these briefs quotes that I have come across from time to time, which I share in all my writings that are important to me, along with a few of my own thoughts.

Life is for the living. Life isn't the destination at the end, but the journey everyone always takes. It's best to live with a little humor in life but be a good soul while down here on solid ground.

I have learned a few important things about myself and I hope you don't mind if I share some of them now.

a. The life that you live is more important than the lifestyle you choose to live.
b. Don't get so busy working to make a living, that you forget to make a life.
c. People (like me and many others) tend to ask G-d for things, like health, wealth, and happiness. I think it would be better to look inwards to yourself and realize that G-d has already bestowed upon us all of these qualities and many more.
d. Don't live your life with regrets. The path untraveled may have given you more happiness than one could ever have imagined.
e. Don't keep all your omissions and fears inside of you. They tend to bog you down and may keep you from the incredible journey your life will become.
f. Live the only life that you have been given. Remember that life is for the living.

I wish you nothing but good health and happiness. Everyone simply wants to live as pain-free a life as possible and leave behind a great legacy for generations to come.

I think that all that people really want is to be loved and be able to love. Reach out to someone, say hello, lend a helping hand, call a family member not just in times of need but at any time.

I think sometimes we think that the world we live in is spinning so far and fast. We all want to see the advancements in medicine, in technology, and many great accomplishments that we sometimes forget.

But we also must not forget to treat our fellow human beings with dignity, compassion, understanding, and civility, no matter who they are, what gender, sexual orientation, race, or religion that they are.

I deal with my own internal and external stress by putting pen to paper and I write down my words in thoughts and quotes. While many of the readers will say that my book may have a few typos, or some incorrect grammar, or thought processes where I digressed, or had too many pictures, quotes, or expressions, I simply say this: I told my story about my experiences the best that I could, nothing more and nothing less.

Life is busy but all in all a wonderful journey of mostly good times to enjoy with occasional bumps along the way.

Life is for the living so live it to the fullest.

"The meaning of life is to find your gift. The purpose of life is to give it away." Pablo Picasso.

I guess my gift is to be at the right place at the right time.

Everyone is busy today and sometimes it seems that life is moving in fast forward.

I called this book that I completed *Right Place, Right Time Part 2*.

I hope that the reader enjoyed reading my stories as they all are true and came from my heart. Some of you may think I made some of them up, but I can honestly say, I did not. Many of the readers have stories to tell but can't, won't, or prefer to keep them private. Whether you believe my stories or not is up to you. I have always told stories, and have still many more to write. I have lived my life to the best of my ability and will continue to do so. I like to say the Journey of one's Life is what's important, and not the Destination that we all will someday unfortunately achieve.

Life is full of surprises; you never know what will happen next. You can be here now and gone in the next minute. Some of my stories may seem funny, harmless, and simple, but certainly not all of them; the worst of any one of them could have happened to me or the person standing next door. You can live a good life by living good, clean, and simple. Don't take too many unnecessary chances that could result in harm, injury, or even death.

Imagine if we all just loved and supported each other for no reason, instead of hating and judging each other for no reason; the world could possibly be a better place for us all.

Imagine that!!!!

We all have turning points in our lives. They may be health issues or a relationship or a career opportunity that we accept or not. Most of the time we can't see them until they are in our rearview mirror (our eyes or our thoughts). I'm here to tell you that now, in any given moment, every one of these choices or intersections offers several possibilities. With the knowledge or the information given to you, one has to pick the right road and sometimes make the choice quickly. Every person has a right to make their own choice in life. It could be as simple as go here or go there. What we need to do is not to reject making any decision. Life is indeed a gift that has been given to you and it's never really over. Life always moves forward; the only thing you need to do is to have Faith, not in anyone else but only in yourself. Do you know what everyone has in common? No one knows what's going to happen next! And that is the END!

ACKNOWLEDGEMENTS

I want to first thank my wonderful granddaughter Maya. While writing this book she always knew when to give me a zinger, tell a joke, or give me a hug. She is a great friend and lover of animals. Whenever I see her, she always lights up the room with her charm and witticisms. I am very lucky and grateful that she is my one and only (and favorite) grandchild and I will always love her.

I also want to thank my son, Jake, whose help in the area of computer issues and Excel spreadsheets was invaluable as I began the arduous process of putting the book together. Jake was always eager to help me with technical issues even when I didn't know those issues existed (although they always did). He gave me a great education in the area of saving documents and the great counsel of backing up everything on my computer as well as on an encrypted thumb drive. For all of these items I say thank you, Jake.

I also want to thank my daughter-in-law Maria who always lent an open ear whenever I had questions and supplied me with her good humor and friendly banter.

I also need to mention my late son Max who passed away at the young age of twenty on February 18, 2004. He dedicated his short life to helping those in need. May his memory be a blessing.

I also dedicated this book to the love of my life, my wife of forty-four-plus years Barbara. She stood by me during this process and always offered kind words and understanding even when I drove her crazy. I always appreciate her witticisms and constructive criticisms whenever they were presented to me. To have someone to love me during all our times together whether they be good or bad is truly a blessing. I can't thank her enough for always standing by my side and I will always cherish her counsel, love, and understanding.

ABOUT THE AUTHOR

Kevin Dwares is a four-time author writing about his life experiences from October 28, 1955 through the present. This book is called *Right Place, Right Time Part 2* and is published by Stillwater Publishing located in West Warwick, Rhode Island. This book, which took many months to complete, consists of fifty-seven true short stories of his life from his birth on October 28, 1955 and is a continuation of his prior book, *Right Place, Right Time*.

Kevin's third book entitled *Right Place, Right Time* was published by Stillwater Publishing located in West Warwick, Rhode Island. This book, which took fifteen months to complete, consists of fifty-four short true stories of his life from his birth on October 28, 1955 until the time of the publication of the book. The stories were accurate and truthful and they had a humorous side as well.

Kevin's second book entitled *A Royal Crowning Achievement* was published by Stillwater Publishing in 2023 located in Pawtucket, Rhode Island. This book took nine months to complete and was about his dental experiences from 2020 to 2022 when he had fourteen dental crowns placed in his mouth. The book details his forty-five appointments and also has a humorous side.

Kevin's first book entitled *Live to the Max* was published in 2016 by the Christian Faith Publishing Company and took fifteen years to complete due to the sensitivity of the subject matter. This book was about the life and faith of his late son Max Gold Dwares who passed away on February 18, 2004 at the age of twenty from complications related to a bone marrow transplant to cure him of leukemia.

Prior to writing his first book, Kevin spent over thirty years as a federal employee in the area of contracting and special project management.

During his spare time, he likes to snowshoe in the mountains, exercise, and spend time traveling around the United States and Israel, which he has visited nine times. Kevin spends time volunteering at food pantries and collecting donations to distribute to local organizations to distribute to the needy.

Kevin volunteers at different places, such as the Rhode Island T.F. Green International Airport in the customer service program that allows members of our community to serve as ambassadors to passengers and visitors. The volunteer program is always in need of more folks to volunteer. Feel free to reach out. Their website is: https://www.flyri.com/riac/volunteer/.

He also volunteers for the Rhode Island Military Organization located at T.F. Green International Airport. This group supports Rhode Island servicemembers and their families via the military lounge located at the airport. Feel free to reach out to them at: http://RIMilitaryOrganization.com.

Another organization he volunteers at is the Tomorrow Fund for Children with Cancer. He has decided once again to donate all proceeds from the sale of *Right Place, Right Time Part 2* to The Tomorrow Fund to help children and their families! Feel free to make a donation to them at:

The Tomorrow Fund
RI Hospital Campus
110 Lockwood Street
Physician's Office Bldg.
Suite 422
Providence, RI 02903
401.444.8811
www.tomorrowfund.org

Kevin's most important time is spent with his thirteen-year-old granddaughter Maya who is named after his late son Max.

Kevin lives in Cranston, Rhode Island with his wife of forty-four years Barbara, his dog Harry, and his cat named Gaby. Kevin's son Jake and his wife Maria and their daughter Maya live less than five minutes away so he visits them frequently. Kevin hopes that this new book entitled *Right Place, Right Time Part 2* will serve as an inspiration to others who have gone through many personal experiences, good or bad, but are unable to discuss them for various reasons. As always, Kevin leaves you with the comments. Remember life is for the living, so always live to the Max (*L'chaim*).

Made in the USA
Middletown, DE
27 March 2025

73309168R00085